GEOGRAPHY BEHIND POLITICS

GEOGRAPHY

Editors

PROFESSOR S. W. WOOLDRIDGE
C.B.E., D.SC., F.R.S.

and

PROFESSOR W. G. EAST
M.A.

Professors of Geography in the University of London

GEOGRAPHY
BEHIND POLITICS

A. E. MOODIE

B.A., PH.D.

*Professor of Geography, Northwestern
University, Illinois, formerly Reader in
Geography in the University of London*

HUTCHINSON UNIVERSITY LIBRARY

LONDON

HUTCHINSON & CO. (*Publishers*) LTD
178–202 Great Portland Street, London, W.1

London Melbourne Sydney
Auckland Bombay Toronto
Johannesburg New York

First published 1949
Second (revised) impression 1957
Third impression 1959
Fourth impression 1961

This book has been set in Imprint type face. It has been printed in Great Britain by The Anchor Press, Ltd., in Tiptree, Essex, on Antique Wove paper and bound by Taylor Garnett Evans & Co., Ltd., in Watford, Herts

CONTENTS

	Preface	6
I	The Scope of Political Geography	7
II	The Evolution of States	19
III	Internal Political Geography	34
IV	Inter-State Relationships	57
V	Frontiers and Boundaries	72
VI	Communications	103
VII	Demographic Aspects	133
VIII	Summary and Conclusions	163
	Index	177

LIST OF MAPS

1	A Decade of Effort—Attempts to settle the Julian Boundary, 1914–24	76
2	Suggested Boundaries in the Julian March 1946–47	77
3	Permanent Villages and Summer Settlements of a part of the Polish Tatra	90
4	Commune Boundaries in a part of the Polish Tatra	91
5	The Piedicolle Section of the Rapallo Line	93
6	Distribution of Net Production Rates in Europe about 1930–35	139

PREFACE

THE author of a book on Political Geography inevitably invites criticism because there are, as yet, no clearly defined and generally accepted limits to its subject matter. Yet there can be no denial of the existence of important relationships between political affairs and the physical environments in which they are set. Quite recently, a Trade Union leader, speaking to a large audience on the relations between Britain and Eastern Europe, said, "You cannot contract out of Geography". However restricted his conception of "Geography" may have been, his statement was indicative of the increasing appreciation of geographical influences in national and international political activities. The difficulty lies in drawing the line between the geographical and the non-geographical. In this respect, I gratefully acknowledge my indebtedness to Professors East and Wooldridge for their assistance, but I must also make clear that the responsibility for opinions expressed in this book rests on me alone.

For the sake of clarity, I have written the word State with a capital initial wherever it refers to a unitary or federated political entity. I have given frequent footnote references in preference to bibliographical lists at the ends of chapters in order to suggest further reading material on specific points.

The Overseas Unit Sales Section of U.N.O. gave me permission to reproduce Figure 6 in a slightly modified form, and Messrs G. Philip and Son, Ltd., have kindly allowed the reproduction of Figures 1 and 5 from my book *The Italo–Yugoslav Boundary* which they published in 1945.

It would be ungracious on my part not to acknowledge with gratitude the help I have received from my wife, both in reading and checking the manuscript and in reading foreign texts.

A. E. MOODIE
London, 1947

I

THE SCOPE OF POLITICAL
GEOGRAPHY

THE political map of the world reveals a distributional pattern of States of various kinds which bear little or no resemblance to the "natural regions" of the geographer. A characteristic feature of all these States is that superficially they possess little in common, yet each represents the organized efforts of its inhabitants to adapt their activities, political and otherwise, to their environmental conditions, with the result that a rather bewildering mosaic confronts the map-reader who may be further embarrassed by the knowledge that the details of his map are liable to change at relatively frequent intervals. Furthermore, the rate and incidence of change vary, in place and in time. States have the quality of mutability in a marked degree.

The field of study of Political Geography is concerned with two basic considerations. First, and of fundamental importance, is the analysis of the relationships between community and physical environment. As all States, by their nature as constituent elements in the world political structure, are connected more or less intimately with other States, these relationships fall into two groups or aspects, the integration of which frequently tests the ability of those who are responsible for policy making. The division into internal and external relationships should not be over-emphasized, but provides a useful line of approach in an analytical treatment. Every organized State has administrative departments comparable with the British Home Office and Foreign Office, and in each case there appears to be inadequate collaboration between these two organs of government, yet their very existence epitomizes the duality of the State's functions. The failure of political leaders to harmonize internal activities with those of the State as a constituent element of the world polity is largely the cause of that disunity and instability which may culminate in global warfare. The division is used here simply for convenience of analysis, but the provision must be made that the overriding necessity of modern times is the integration of both internal and external State relationships.

The entire land surface of the earth, with its great wealth of geographical environments, is now shared by a large number of States which do not conform to any clearly defined type, but each of which possesses three essential elements, territory, people, and organizations, which may be analysed, described and mapped with considerable accuracy. But wherever people live on a territory and whatever political system they may adopt, their activities represent, at least in part, a response to environmental conditions which, in their turn, set limits to and affect those human activities which take place within the territorial framework.

No State can exist *in vacuo*, without a territory, but no territory can be formed into a State without people. There may be "Stateless persons", but there can be no uninhabited States, although some modern political units include areas of very low population densities. Thus the twin pillars of the State, territory and people, are closely welded together by their relationships. This is no mere "geographical determinism". There is no guarantee that the people inhabiting a State territory will react to its environmental conditions in a given manner: hence the great variety of political and economic organizations which exist, and will probably continue to exist, in the world. What can be said in general terms of this aspect of Political Geography is that every environment provides certain opportunities which its inhabitants may or may not utilize, which may lie dormant and unappreciated until an appropriate phase in the development of the people has been reached.

The extent to which environmental opportunities are realized and utilized is reflected in the success and stability of the economic techniques and political forms of a particular State, but it does not follow that the methods and forms of one State will be equally applicable to another set of environmental conditions. One of the most useful conclusions to be derived from politico-geographical studies is the unwisdom of imposing systems which have proved successful in one case no other States, more especially in the political sphere.

Every modern State, then, represents an amalgam of three elements, territory, people, and the relationships between them. The first two are of great variety, but the third element is of infinite complexity, nowhere capable of being reduced to mathematical formulæ but everywhere possessing a dynamic quality inasmuch as these relationships are subject to unceasing change and development. Clearly the study of every aspect of these three elements is beyond the scope of Political Geography. The art of government deals with one branch of State activities and, it may be added, its practitioners often show a lamentable ignorance not only of the relationships between environment and people but also of these two elements themselves. The physical environment falls largely within the purview of Physical Geography, while the distributions of populations and their varying densities are the field of study of Demography. Historians, economists, sociologists and psychologists all have their interests in one or more of the essential elements of the State.

While recognizing the work and contributions of all these branches of study, as well as of many others, the student of Political Geography justly claims a wider field. He sees each State as an entity with its characteristic features welded together by its internal relationships, but, at the same time, he also sees it as a part of a greater framework which is the world in which we live and the symbiotic character of which, in virtue of the relationships between its component parts, he recognizes and seeks to analyse.

This recognition of the dualism of the State, as a whole and as a part of a greater entity, is one of the differentiating factors between Political Geography and other disciplines. In no case is there a sharply marked dividing line between the internal and external functioning of the State; the two sets of relationships are indeed closely connected. The stage of development reached by the internal relationships, the smoothness with which they work, and the well-being of the human element in the State will inevitably affect its external relationships.

Conversely, unsatisfactory external relationships may disturb internal conditions to the point where they become intolerable to the inhabitants and force them to adopt a line of action which, under other circumstances, might appear to be impossible. In fine, the immediate environment of any State only exists within a larger, more widely-spread, environment of which it is a part. If the aim of statesmen should be to harmonize the relationships of the community with these two closely related sets of environmental conditions, that of the political geographer is to analyse and put on record those geographical bases of human relationships without which societies cannot exist.

The second basic consideration in Political Geography is that States are subject to change, more particularly during periods such as the present century, which may well prove to be the greatest time of experimentation in the world's history. This susceptibility to change is by no means restricted to the internal conditions of the State, but extends to its external relationships, and although the concept of change is no recent discovery, there can be no doubt that the tempo of present-day activities has greatly increased above and beyond that of preceding times. Perhaps the chief result is an increasing awareness of the relationships between communities and their environments, with an associated refinement of human adaptations which is sometimes loosely described as the "Conquest of Nature".

Such a phrase is far from being accurate, in spite of the remarkable achievements which have been made in many directions. Yet it must be admitted that mankind is within reach of conditions by which at least his material wants may be satisfied to an extent which has never before been possible. Millions of Chinese people may still starve every year, and the material well-being of other millions in India cannot be said to have reached a satisfactory level, but even in these extreme cases improved transport facilities and organizational powers have brought about some alleviation. It is no facile optimism to hope that further changes in agricultural and industrial activities may facilitate the development of better standards of living in regions where hitherto the welfare of the community as a whole has received little attention.

Whatever the motive forces behind them, these changes

are important if for no other reason than that they are accompanied by widespread developments in political and economic thought which inevitably influence both the internal and external relationships of States. If peace is indivisible so are the external relationships of States, and they, in their turn, cannot be completely separated from internal conditions. A drought in North America has its repercussions in Europe; a "White Australian Policy" may foster militarism in Japan, and the rapid spread of warfare from its point or region of origin is all too familar to be stressed here.

Similarly, ideas, whether of a moral, political or economic character, cannot be isolated within the confines of any one State. Never before has there existed such a multiplicity of channels of communications. The invention of the printing-press certainly assisted the propagation of ideas, and its results are still important, but the possible effects of the radio and of the cinema are beyond assessment at present. Even India, with its hundreds of millions of illiterates, already possesses its own film studios, native actors and actresses, and cinemas in most of its urban centres. The effects, direct and indirect, of such a phenomenal growth, not by any means confined to one State or to any part of the earth, are still incalculable but the possibilities are enormous.

This background of "ferment and change" cannot be ignored by the political geographer because it forms part of the environment in which people live and, as such, will exert a directive influence on the forms of States and on the character of inter-State relations. Increasing knowledge is not necessarily coterminous with increasing wisdom, but increasing access to knowledge, now possible without the medium of the written word, may lead to the growth of desires and demands which, by accelerating the rate of change, may modify the forms and functions of States to a degree beyond our present comprehension.

Twenty-seven years ago an eminent geographer wrote, " . . . a national society can be shaped to a desired career while it is young, but when it is old its character is fixed and it is incapable of any great change in its mode of existence".[1] In

[1] Sir Halford Mackinder, *Democratic Ideals and Reality*, London, 1919, p. 12.

the light of the events and changes which have taken place since those words were written, is it possible to make such an assertion today? Russia was an "old" State in 1919 yet what changes in "its mode of existence" have taken place since that date! Political unity may seem to be impossible of achievement in present-day China, but any prophecy regarding the major events of the next twenty years in that country will almost certainly prove to be inaccurate.

The essential fact for the political geographer, as indeed for the politician and the historian, is that States and their relationships change with changing conditions of human existence in the widest sense. Not even the geographical framework itself remains permanently unaltered; in virtue of the persistent and continued efforts of mankind to adapt its means of existence to environmental conditions, the very landscape suffers modifications. Much greater is the rate of change in the political organization of societies, both internally and externally, yet even this tempo has not been able to keep pace with economic changes. There seems to be a time lag between the development of political and economic systems; changes in the latter occur first because they represent, in general, mankind's primary function of providing itself with the basic necessities of life—food, clothing, shelter, etc., whereas political changes generally follow at a later stage because one of the main functions of the political structure of a State is to organize and facilitate the economic activities of its inhabitants.

If the politician and the economist, then, must recognize this concept of changing conditions in a changing world, together with all its implications, the political geographer is concerned with the observation, recording and analysis of the changes which have already taken place, as well as of those which are proceeding at the present time.

In the light of the above, it becomes plain that Political Geography is an aspect of the even wider study known as Human Geography, but it possesses an all-important differentiating element which gives it a specialist character. Human Geography deals with the relationships between societies and their physical environments without any necessary restriction to the particular political forms which they may take. Thus the areal unit of the human geographer is generally the geographical region, large or small, which is regarded as a "natural" entity possessing an individuality arising out of the symbiosis of physical and human elements which, in its turn, makes the region clearly recognizable although the precise delimitation of its boundaries may be difficult or even impossible.

On the other hand, the areal unit of the political geographer is the State, which is more or less artificial in so far as it is the product of the conscious efforts of its inhabitants to create a political entity which may be, and usually is, entirely different from the geographical region. In practice, mankind has so far shown a complete inability to devise a pattern of States to coincide with the "natural" pattern suggested by the geographer's regions. The political map of Europe, for example, illustrates the conflict particularly well. From a geographical point of view, there is much to be said for including the southern shorelands of the Mediterranean Sea in the continent of Europe. Again, the eastern boundary of Europe has no reality in the spheres of politics and economics and is not even an internal administrative boundary in the U.S.S.R. The Middle Danubian Basin indicates an admirable framework for a single State, yet it is divided among several political entities between which there seems to be little hope of union.

Many similar examples are to be found, not only in Europe, but in other parts of the world, and they all point to the same conclusion. In his overriding desire to establish and maintain States man has largely ignored the possible framework of geographical regions; in his efforts to secure the integrity of States he has been compelled to impose arbitrary political boundaries concerning which inter-State relations are frequently in conflict.

The areas with which Political Geography deals are therefore clearly defined and clearly demarcated. With all their great variety of size, shape and content, they represent artificial creations and, as such, must be recognized as realities in a world where the real and the unreal are all too often confused. The point is worth making, however, that in being concerned with States, the political geographer has the great advantage of having access to statistical material of many kinds and which are compiled on a State basis. The students of Regional and Human Geography are frequently embarrassed by being unable to obtain statistical evidence of their deductions because no adequate machinery exists for the collection of similar data regarding geographical regions. Because of the nature of the political organization of States and for administrative purposes, censuses and the like must be compiled for areas within political boundaries. Hence the study of Political Geography is facilitated and made more exact by the availability of collected statistical material without which arguments cannot be fully supported.

This is not to suggest that the scope of Political Geography is narrow. On the contrary, the great variety of States and the infinite complexity of both their internal and external relationships demand a breadth of outlook which can be founded only on wide knowledge which is only now becoming available, and which is by no means yet complete. At the same time, and if false deductions are to be avoided, the study of Political Geography also requires a high degree of objectivity and detachment; in short, it requires a scientific attitude of mind on the part of its exponents, who must weigh carefully the available evidence and avoid rash generalizations. There are no two identical environments nor are there any two identically similar States in the world. There are no known and exact laws to govern the relationships of peoples and their environments. Certain general tendencies are observable, but even the undeniable force of the urge to acquire the means of existence may be subordinated to other motives, as the various resistance movements in occupied European countries during the recent war amply demonstrated.

It follows, therefore, that Political Geography can never become an exact science and it would be a mistake to suppose that its problems are as susceptible to solution as those of the "pure" sciences. Nevertheless, valid deductions can be made by the objective student who is willing to use the techniques of observation, recording and analysis which have become characteristic of modern geographical studies. This is a high standard to expect, but any deviation from the objective attitude will almost certainly lead to error and confusion. Such a pitfall inevitably awaited the exponents of "Geopolitik" in pre-war Germany, Italy and Japan.

Objectivity should be the guiding light of the political geographer. There is no easy road to the solution of problems of the State, neither within its internal political framework nor in inter-State relations. Indeed the statement of such problems is often a difficult task, especially as the use of the word "problems" suggests that solutions are available. Professor Azcárate, with his detailed knowledge and personal experience of international affairs, lays emphasis on this point. "As though the 'problem' of minorities (or any problem of a political or social nature) were as susceptible of solution as those of physics and mathematics,"[1] he writes. Ways of living, modes of thought, adaptations to physical conditions, are the outcome of experiment, of trial and error, and can be accurately assessed only when regarded objectively and with detachment. While not necessarily permanent nor unchangeable, they must be recognized as existing.

Furthermore, political societies require the right to formulate and operate their own systems provided they do not imperil the survival of other societies. This degree of tolerance must precede any effort to integrate the diverse and disparate political systems of the world; it is an essential prerequisite which is all too frequently overlooked, and never more so than by the believers in Geopolitik which reached its zenith in Germany between the two world wars. They committed the fatal error of subordinating means to the end of German hegemony. Their outlook and literature were entirely subjective and represented a prostitution of the methods and results of Political Geography. This was all the more unfortunate in that many German university teachers and research workers devoted much time and energy to the task of discovering evidence in support of the false Nazi doctrines.

It is to be hoped that these baseless myths have been destroyed, but Geopolitik, in attempting to give a scientific

[1] P. de Azcárate, *League of Nations and National Minorities*, Washington, 1945, p. vii.

colour to spurious theories, rendered a disservice to politico-geographical thought, which is all the more regrettable as it was a German, Ratzel, who was the first among modern writers to study Political Geography along scientific lines. "C'est Ratzel qui, le premier, comprit la complexité des conditions d'existence et de fonctionnement des États et qui sut donner à leur étude le caractère d'une science," wrote Professor Demangeon.[1] This eminent French geographer has no doubts as to the aims of Geopolitik.

> "Nous devons constater que la géopolitique al emande renonce délibérément à tout esprit scientifique. Depuis Ratzel, elle n'a pas progressé; elle a devié sur le terrain des controverses et des haines nationales. Il fut un temps où tous les géographes d'Europe écoutaient ce que leur venait d'Allemagne comme la voix même de la science. Ce temps est revolu, s'il est démontré qui désormais la vérité varie selon les patries . . . la géopolitique est un 'coup monté', une machine de guerre. Si elle veut compter parmi les sciences, il est temps qu'elle revienne à la géographie politique".[2]

Such a scathing denunciation is justified. Its value lies in the fact that it is a warning to all political geographers to walk warily when examining State relationships.

How far the geopolitical researches and writings of Haushofer[3] and his associates influenced recent German efforts to establish a new world order is not yet clear, but there can be no doubt that there was a close connection between Geopolitik and political thinking and planning in pre-war Germany. Much of the published literature contains sufficient factual material, frequently illustrated by striking maps and diagrams, to give the reader an impression of veracity and plausibility which is all too often incorrect. But the basic

[1] A. Demangeon, "Géographie politique", Annales de Géographie, Tome XLI, 1932, p.23.
[2] Ibid., p.31.
[3] See German Strategy of World Conquest, by D. Whittlesey, New York, 1942, for a list of German writings on Geopolitik. For the student who is unable to read German, this book contains a valuable collection of translated quotations from Haushofer and his associates.

error underlying the whole theory of Geopolitik seems to lie in the misinterpretation of the time factor. All States, as well as the political world order, are the results of historical evolution. To a varying extent, they represent an inheritance from the past and, at least in part, they are rooted in the past.

This ought not to suggest that over-emphasis should be placed on past achievements. Often, and especially in the case of European States, "too much history is remembered", and efforts to revive the greatness and glory of an earlier time have led to dismal failures, as recent events in Italy prove only too well.

Again, too much remembered history leads to a rigidity of outlook, and fosters an unwillingness to change shapes and boundaries of States, with a resultant liability to friction and clashes. By realizing and appreciating the continuity of the development of political units, in whatever form they may take, it is possible to grasp the fact that any new system must be grafted on to a pre-existing stock. There can be no absolutely fresh start in these matters. Any attempt to impose a new order, regardless of past and present conditions, implies a misinterpretation of historical events as well as a failure to understand political patterns and relationships. The Germans not only misjudged the timing of their attempted world conquest, but assessed wrongly the forces of cohesion and resistance which proved too successful for them. Their subjectivity, stronger but more blind than Mussolini's *sacro egoismo*, prevented them from developing a balanced outlook on their own conditions and those of other States; they appear to have been lacking in a sense of perspective in time and space.

The evolution of the existing forms of States and of State relationships is properly the sphere of Historical Geography. Studies in Political Geography are primarily concerned with present conditions, but, in view of the weight of past events in modifying what exists today, there is inevitably some overlap of the two fields of investigation. No satisfactory analysis of the internal and external relationships of States can be made independently of knowledge of the previous conditions. No clear-cut dividing line can be drawn between

Historical and Political Geography. Whereas the former deals with the relationships between peoples and environments at various stages in the past, the latter is chiefly concerned with those present-day conditions which may be regarded as a phase in the dynamic evolution of States. Its major objective is the analysis of inter-State relationships and of internal adaptations to environmental conditions. It does not set out to formulate or control State or inter-State policies, but the results achieved by politico-geographical studies, when taken in conjunction with the results from other fields of investigation, can scarcely be ignored by statesmen. While seeking to promote understanding of political forces and systems by making its own distinctive contribution from its own restricted viewpoint, it does not attempt to confuse means with ends under a mantle of slogans and myths which have little or no foundation in fact.

II

THE EVOLUTION OF STATES

THE two and a half billion inhabitants of the earth live in a large number of States, over seventy of which are more or less independent but vary widely in shape, area, population and system of government. All these States, in spite of their diversity, are alike in one respect, that they are founded upon the necessity of political organization of some type or other. Hence the State represents the efforts of its people to organize their activities, and the expression of these attempts to organize is seen in the formulation and application of regulations or laws which are usually codified in some constitutional form. The essential feature of such systems of laws is that they are, at least in theory, formulated by the community as a whole, functioning through the legislative, executive and judicial bodies, and are considered as superior to the regulations evolved by all other associations within the State.

The actual processes in law-making and execution are the field of study of legal experts and can have no place here, but the important fact for the political geographer is that the activities of the people in a State are conditioned by the relationships which exist between the physical or geographical *milieu* and its human inhabitants. It follows, therefore, that the State does not consist of the territory alone, nor of the people who live in that territory, but is a much more complex organization in which the territory, the people and their inter-relationships are indissolubly welded to form an entity which possesses an individuality, a character, which marks it off from all other States.

The visible evidence of this political unity is shown in the degree of common consent in the acceptance of the laws evolved by the governmental agencies of the State; where large sections of the community refuse to accept the system of government working through the legal code there anarchy exists. Where a State is set up in defiance of the relationships between the people and their environment there can be no political stability. The only valid reason for the existence of a State is that it should facilitate the smooth working of those relationships. The State cannot therefore be an end in itself— it can only be a means to an end, and, as such, it must be subject to change with increasing knowledge and with increasing power of the human element over the physical.

Regarded from this angle, the State is largely an artificial creation in so far as it represents the efforts of its inhabitants to develop a framework within which their activities, both internal and external, can be organized and regulated to bring about the maximum benefits for the community. It is a political entity, clearly if arbitrarily defined, and coincident with an area of territory. Rarely, if ever, is the area or space identifiable with a geographical region so that the part of the earth's surface occupied by a State usually lacks homogeneity in geological structure, physiography or climatic conditions. Probably this is to the advantage of the State, because variety of rock type, of land forms and of climate gives rise to a diversity of local and regional environments which may result in a greater wealth of material resources than would be found in a monotonously uniform region. Provided that regional differentiations and the concomitant resources are recognized and catered for in the political organization, they can be integrated in such a way that the best interests of the inhabitants are served. This does not mean that a State must occupy a continuous area of land. A clearly recognized and defined territorial area must be its basis, but it may consist of water-divided areas, such as archipelagos, and, since the sea no longer acts as a major barrier to human movement, it may be composed of more widely separated areas such as those once found in the Venetian Republic or in the modern French Union. While some States occupy small compact land areas, others are spread over large parts of the earth's surface.

In brief, there are no rigid physical criteria for the shape and geographical character of States. The only standard of judgment of the maturity of a State is the extent to which its sovereignty, through the functioning of its power to make and implement laws, is willingly accepted by its human element. It may be argued that this is no concern of the geographer, but inasmuch as the stability, smooth working and successful exploitation of environmental resources are largely dependent on the acceptance of the "rule of law", it follows that human adaptations to environmental conditions are at least closely associated with the political organization of the State, and if Geography is to be anything more than Physiography, the exponent of the former must take cognisance of this aspect of human affairs.[1]

From what has already been said it will be apparent that a rigid physical classification of States is impossible because of the great variety resulting, in part at least, from the diversity of the earth's surface. Moreover, the territorial extent of States, with associated changes in boundaries and material resources, fluctuates. The contemporary pattern of States is different from that of the past and will be different again in the future. This is one answer to those who postulate a narrow determinism. If States were simply and solely the outcome of purely physical conditions, then the scope of human endeavour would be intolerably limited and man would indeed be cabined and confined.

A more reasonable view is that of the State as the temporary result of a long evolutionary process, in which the co-ordination of human activities with the physical background becomes closer, through the medium of ever-increasing experience which itself is aggregated in the social heritage. To deny the value and purpose of the directive power of mankind, however ineffective it may appear to be at times, is to ignore the facts of history. Hence a survey of States, as they exist in the world today, must take into account what has happened in the past, but can be fruitful only when considered as a statement of the present arrangements which, in their turn, will give way

---

[1] It is interesting to notice, in this connection, that Professor van Valkenburg begins his chapter on "Government" by stating that, "The Author is fully aware that a chapter on government does not blend well into a geographical survey. Nevertheless, the type of government of a country is a definite factor in a political-geographical evaluation, for it greatly affects a state's relations with other states."—S. van Valkenburg, *Elements of Political Geography*, New York, 1939, p.302.

to other patterns in the future. Expressed in another way, the present world order is the outcome of long ages of human experiment, which has by no means been always consciously projected towards a uniform objective. Perhaps an outstanding characteristic of our times is the increasing awareness of the existence of a world order of sorts, and a growing belief that this order may be bettered to the benefit of mankind as a whole.

From earliest times in human history man has been impelled to seek the companionship and society of his fellows in some kind of group. Social anthropologists have yet to reach full agreement concerning the economies of these early societies, but man's gregarious habit was developed from the first, probably as the result of a combination of instinct and acquired characteristics. Man not only finds it agreeable to live in groups; he derives material advantages from association with his fellows. Greater security is obtained, and gradually, by division of labour, easement of life's economic burdens may be secured.

On the other hand, association in groups throws up individuals who reveal powers of leadership and seek to impose their wills on their associates, thus tending to bind together the community. Prowess acquired in combat or as a result of greater skill in the direction of affairs gives added power to the leader, who is therefore able to combine his subordinates by the enforcement of regulations for the conduct of life as well as by his own personal inspiration. Group organization, therefore, is developed at a primitive level but is of a more complex character than is usually allowed, as investigations into the conduct of existing primitive peoples indicate.

From these first beginnings of organized social life, based largely on personal contacts, gradually evolved the early civilizations, assisted by the natural growth of population combined with increasing skill in the provision of the material needs of life, but often as the result of superior military strength which made possible the imposition of control by a numerically inferior group on a larger aggregation of peoples. With the development of sedentary agriculture and its associated domestic industries and commerce, the inhabited earth became more productive, societies became more closely tied to the territories with which they identified themselves, and a tendency to agglomeration on the part of the peoples gave rise to early urban growth, more particularly as the circulation of goods and people became focussed at selected points which possessed nodality.

In this way the first City States grew up, and military conquest was then able to lead to amalgamation, as in the case of ancient Greece, and later to the establishment of so-called Empires. Once the idea of territorial expansion was successfully implemented, its corollary of internal organization demanded attention in so far as the newly acquired territory could not be held together except by the establishment of lines of communication nor could it be defended against external attack or internal disintegration without these vital arteries.

Here it is possible to discern the first great political States with their threefold elements, people, territory and organization, and best exemplified in the case of the Roman Empire. Then, as now, the level of organization, that is to say the skill, initiative and ingenuity of joint human adaptations to the physical environment, was the differentiating factor as between States. People and territory had long been in existence, but the decisive factor in the success or failure of the Ancient Empires was the part played by their inhabitants in organizing relationships, both among themselves and between themselves, and the physical environment in which they lived. It is significant in this connection that the Ancient Greeks were among the first to formulate theories of the State and that Political Science as well as Political Geography first received serious attention from their wise men.

The Dark Ages were dark primarily because the established system of political organization, as far as Europe was concerned, broke down under the impact of a politically unorganized series of invasions by relatively backward peoples. Yet they were only a prelude to a further phase in the evolution of States and, as such, showed glimpses of efforts to achieve State organizations which some historians regard as the foundations of later developments. Throughout that long period, societies continued to exist but lacked any centralized control because systems of communication had collapsed. Inevitably, close personal ties dominated human relationships, as exemplified in the Feudal System, largely because contact with a central authority was either impossible or unworkably slow. By means of a long series of conflicts during the Middle Ages, personal relationships with local leaders were replaced by attachments to dynasties, frequently bolstered up by such doctrines as divine rights of kings and so forth.

Throughout both these Ages the leadership principle appears to have been universally accepted, and with it the concept of the leader as the source of law and power. The political history of the Modern Age is largely the story of the successful struggle to wrest this omnicompetence from an individual or from a privileged few and, through the growth of Parliamentary Government and the extension of the franchise, to bestow self-government. The process is by no means complete yet and many are the ways by which different societies are still striving to build satisfying political organizations. It would be unwise to regard the modern State as having reached perfection, or to think of it as having reached a stage of finality, yet it is true that, under its ægis, man is freer from the inhibiting restrictions of the physical environment than he has ever been in the past.

Having briefly traced the evolution of the modern State, attention may now be drawn to certain of its outstanding characteristics. Above all else, the modern State is a sovereign State, that is to say it holds supreme sway over the territory and the people (with certain minor reservations) within its limits, and in this respect is not answerable to any other authority. It is therefore completely independent politically. For the political geographer, the sovereignty of the State is interesting mainly because of the ways in which the sovereign power is employed to direct and control both the internal and external relationships of its inhabitants. It is clear that the influence of a State, at least in external affairs, depends on the power which the State has at its absolute command. The fact that the commonest classification of States is into Great Powers and Small Powers is evidence of the overwhelming importance of power, both military and economic, although the two can scarcely be separated in these days of highly organized industrialism.

There is no clear-cut dividing line between the two kinds of Powers and recent events have demonstrated that a Great Power may be reduced to a lower status by the effects, for example, of war. The power of any State cannot be said to rest on any one material element, but rather it depends on the degree of organization of all the available resources, both material and spiritual. Thus Russia, impoverished and helpless as a result of its participation in the First World War, temporarily ceased to be considered as a Great Power. Clearly great area alone is not an adequate basis for the claim to be reckoned as a Great Power, but when the resources of a large State are mobilized and organized, then that State may justly claim to rank among the leading Powers. When great area is combined with great resources, and particularly when such materially well-endowed territory is densely populated with energetic people with a high net reproductive rate, then the State which controls this combination is indeed a Great Power.

Nevertheless, it is important to stress the fact that the greatness of the State depends ultimately on the degree of organization in all spheres of activity with which it is concerned. Once that organization breaks down, through whatever cause, then the State inevitably loses stature. State power then is primarily a function of organization. That is what differentiates the modern State from all its predecessors. That is why the will and capacity to organize are fundamental in all States worthy of that title.

It will be apparent, however, that no amount of organizing capacity will be valuable in the absence of resources, in the form of material and human wealth, to organize. Small States are therefore faced with an alternative choice. They can either be content to remain small and relatively powerless, or they must expand. The Great Powers have all achieved their greatness by choosing the latter alternative at some time or other, that is to say they have all either passed through, or are attempting to pass through now, a phase of expansionism in order to acquire greater territory or resources upon which to organize their power. The methods employed have varied. In the past, the simplest and most widely practised was to annex either adjacent or more distant territory, more particularly in areas where the special needs of the State could be satisfied, either in the supply of materials or in the establishment of markets. Typical examples are to be found in the growth of the British Empire, the westward expansion of U.S.A., and the incorporation of what is now called Soviet Asia in the present U.S.S.R.

Such forms of expansionism were possible because of the relative lack of resistance in the newly acquired lands and, be it noted, resistance was absent largely because of inefficient organization. Where resistance was met, the expansionist States employed other devices, not least of which was military conquest and occupation, and frequently mercantile concessions were extracted. There is a limit to this type of expansionism which appears to have been reached. The world's "empty spaces" have been occupied in the sense that they have been incorporated in the territory controlled by States and, henceforward, territorial expansion can only be achieved by means of warfare.

Against this, however, it must be admitted that there is still a kind of economic imperialism whereby States seek to acquire control of materials and markets by manipulations of monetary systems and diverse other means. The present outcome of all these expansionist tendencies and efforts is that a small number of States possess the rank, influence and prestige of Great Powers while the remainder are strung out in an order of decreasing world importance, but, great and small, they each claim to be sovereign and therefore legally equal, whereas any realistic approach to the study of their relationships must take into account their inequality in power and wealth.

The growth of the State in its modern form has been closely associated with the evolution of nationalism, so much so indeed that frequently "State" and "nation" are used as interchangeable terms, often leading to confusion of thought and meaning. As has already been shown, the State is composed of territory and people bound together by organization on a political level. Statehood is only achieved when the inhabitants of a territory are united under one government. Nationality, on the other hand, may and does exist independently of a form of political organization and may spread beyond the territorial limits of a given State. While the distinguishing feature of members of a State is that they owe allegiance to a sovereign power, the members of a nation are united by a feeling of "belonging together" although they may be separated by political boundaries. In short, the State is a political community, whereas the nation is characterized by cultural ties, most frequently expressed in the possession of a common language.

Where there is identity of nation and State, there the National State is said to exist, but a cursory examination of existing conditions will show that multi-national States are by no means uncommon. Even in such small territories as Great Britain and Belgium, if there are not distinct nations, distinctive national elements are to be found, while in larger States, for example the U.S.S.R., there may be many nationalities. Fortunate is the State, therefore, which has no "nationality problems", but even more fortunate is the State which, in virtue of the wise working of its political system, has successfully overcome the disruptive tendencies of national differences which at one time existed within its present limits.

The territorial and omnicompetent State may be the offspring of the religious struggles of the sixteenth century, as Professor Laski argues,[1] but its present-day character is largely the result of conscious human efforts to establish political entities. Nations, on the other hand, develop out of long periods of natural growth during which bonds of custom, language and religion are forged. The national group is certainly related to a more or less defined territory, but which does not possess clear-cut boundaries, since human movement was unrestricted until the establishment of modern State limits. Once the concept of the all-powerful State became accepted, the necessity arose of reconciling State and nation and, in general, areas occupied by people of one nationality have become co-extensive with State territories. In many cases, however, people who considered themselves as belonging to one nation did not occupy continuous areas. When States were

[1] H. J. Laski, *A Grammar of Politics*, London, 1925, p.45.

set up, therefore, there were frequently "outliers" of nationality which could not be easily included in their national State without obvious injustice to the other nationals among whom they lived. Similar but more complex difficulties arose in regions of mixed nationalities where the establishment of political boundaries inevitably outraged national feelings and gave rise to that discontent and friction which are the bases of "Minority Problems".

Few States are entirely uninational and to that extent the term National State is a misnomer, but since nationalism is considered to be a powerful factor in the unifying processes of the State, it has been deliberately encouraged in many cases, even to the extent of attempted imposition of so-called national uniformity. But habits of thought and language, customs and creeds, because they are the resultants of many generations of growth, are not easily eradicated, either by the use of force or by intensive propaganda.

There is nothing inherently wrong in nationalism. As Professor Chadwick says:[1]

> "Nationalism is no doubt a vivifying and inspiring force. It makes for national unity and—when it is genuine and not merely a cloak for political ambitions—it acts as a curb upon the selfish instincts of individuals and of classes and professions. Its ugly side appears only when it is associated with aggression against neighbouring states, or with the coercion of alien or dissentient elements at home."

If the world patterns of States and nations were completely identical there would be fewer problems in the administration of world affairs, but, short of widespread transfers of populations to such an extent that existing States and nations became everywhere identified, it is possible to lessen at least some of the difficulties in one of two ways. In Europe, where the nationalities problem is most acute, attempts were made in the interwar period to implement the principle of self-determination whereby new States were established on the basis of nationality.

In this way Czechoslovakia and Jugoslavia came into

[1] H. M. Chadwick, *The Nationalities of Europe and the Growth of National Ideologies*, Cambridge, 1945, p.7

existence, Poland was revived, and a number of adjustments
were made between State territories and areas largely inhabited
by people of common nationality. A great deal of careful
consideration and endeavour was put into the new arrangements. Territorial transfers alone entailed a tremendous
amount of investigation and organization, as Miss Sophia
Saucerman has shown.[1] In particular, the Middle Zone of
Europe was completely reorganized, but there still remained
some national minorities. The net result was an increase in
the number of politically independent States, not all of which
contained sufficient inhabitants with adequate political wisdom
and experience to conduct either their external or their internal
affairs satisfactorily. In the upshot, the new States proved
too weak to withstand the aggression of more powerful neighbours and, for a time, lost their independence.

Furthermore, it seems that, having recovered their earlier
political status, they are still lacking in those resources which
would enable them to survive without the assistance of one
or more Great Powers. This may entail infringements of their
sovereign rights.[2] On the whole, it appears that multiplication
of States, whether on the grounds of nationality or of any other
common interests, is unwise, especially in a continent such as
Europe, where space is not unlimited, and where material
resources may be better utilized under the aegis of a smaller
number of political organizations. A more successful way of
easing the difficulties of nationalities may be found in grouping
them together as States with adequate economic resources,
but within which each nationality should retain a considerable
degree of at least cultural autonomy.[3] This method has been

[1] S. Saucerman, *International Transfers of Territory in Europe*, Washington,
1937.

[2] Professor E. H. Carr goes further than this when he says, "The small
country can survive only by seeking permanent association with a Great
Power." cf. *Conditions of Peace*, London, 1944, p.55.

[3] On this point, Professor Azcárate, who has had wide practical experience
of investigating minority problems, writes, "The crisis of the classic formula,
'Every nation a state and every state a nation', is now perceptible; there are
manifold indications that Europe is moving towards the establishment of
new political forms based on wider political concentrations (states), within
which the 'nations' will find appropriate conditions for the preservation and
development of national values." cf. *League of Nations and National Minorities*,
Washington, 1945, p. 8. viii.

applied in the U.S.S.R. with considerable success, as far as can be judged, although it is only fair to point out that the background of nationality problems in that State is different from that in Central Europe.

The exponents of national self-determination, more particularly in the years which immediately followed the end of the First World War, were doubtless possessed of high ideals, and at least those who were not intimately familiar with such areas as Central and Eastern Europe showed a considerable degree of altruism. But they appear to have overlooked the fact that the so-called rights of nationality carry obligations in their train. Nowhere is this more apparent than in the sphere of economic affairs. Whereas the hallmark of the political State is its sovereign power and consequent independence, and experience shows that any infringement of this sovereignty will be met with resistance, either open or clandestine, yet the world as a whole is becoming increasingly interdependent in the economic sense. Herein lies a dilemma which contains the roots of many obstacles to the achievement of world peace and prosperity.

Because of its complete autonomy, the State has the right, under existing conditions, to formulate and execute its own economic policy, and there is no known method, not even that of war, of coercing it into co-operation with other States in economic matters, yet such co-operation is one of the outstanding needs of the world at the present time and will probably remain so for a long time to come.

It may be argued again that this is no concern of the political geographer, yet the position must be recognized if any rational appreciation of inter-State relationships is to be reached. The need is all the more urgent in view of the development of what has been called economic nationalism which aims at making the State as independent economically as it is politically. Carried to extreme lengths, its objective is economic autarchy or self-sufficiency which can be fully achieved only by divorcing the State from all external resources.

Since no political unit contains adequate supplies of all the necessary ingredients of material well-being for its people, and since synthetic methods of production are usually more costly than what may be termed "natural" methods, complete economic nationalism tends to result in the lowering of standards of living. It is therefore a retrogressive system, exerting an adverse effect sooner or later on the inhabitants of the would-be self-sufficient State, but also acting as a brake on the full development of world trade. Some measure of the desirability, if not the absolute necessity, of furthering economic co-operation between States and, by implication, the need of abandoning economic autarchy, is provided by the recent establishment of the Economic and Social Council of U.N.O. and it may be worth recalling that the fourth "principle" of the Atlantic Charter is:

> "They [President Roosevelt and Mr. Winston Churchill] will endeavour, with due respect for their existing obligations, to further enjoyment by all States, great or small, victor or vanquished, of access, on equal terms, to the trade and to the raw materials of the world which are needed for their economic prosperity."

Clearly the evolution of States has reached a critical stage, and this crisis is, in no small degree, to be associated with the rapid growth of nationalism in all its forms, but more particularly since the middle of the nineteenth century. Equally clearly, that rapid growth has in its turn been related to the swift development and spread of industrialization, not because all States are highly industrialized, but because the development of industrial communities, usually in the form of high demographic concentrations, has fostered world trade and world communications to such an extent that even States which are primarily agricultural feel the repercussions of the struggle for materials and markets between competing industrial countries. There is no disguising the fact that the conflict lies between the political independence of States, on the one hand, and their economic interdependence, on the other. The problem may be stated in its simplest form as a question. Can the sovereign State, irrespective of its size and power, share fully in the world's resources, and thus improve the material well-being of its people, and still retain its political independence? Economic nationalism certainly provides no generally acceptable answer to this all-important question, and the international system, based on diplomacy, treaties and agreements, does not appear to have found a way of reconciling the difficulties of production, consumption and distribution on a world scale as the events of the inter-war period indicated.

What is required is a universally accepted plan for the organization of production and consumption, but such a scheme implies some sacrifice of sovereignty on the part of each and every State, and the available evidence suggests that this is precisely the course which most States are not yet willing to follow. This is not to suggest that the position is completely hopeless. It would be folly to expect all the States to abandon overnight the principles on which they have been founded. Changes in outlook in both the internal and in the external affairs of the State must take time, and rightly so, if conflicts are to be avoided. Yet there are already indications that the peoples of the world are being converted to the necessity of greater inter-State co-operation. The League of Nations was not a complete failure. Some of its achievements, especially in connection with the International Labour Organization, and perhaps less creatively in the Minorities Disputes, were of lasting benefit, and its successor, the United Nations Organization, while previously concerned with the immediate effects of war at this stage, has considerable powers to deal with economic and social problems.

The very title of the latest grouping suggests that its sponsors are aware of the urgent necessity to organize world relationships, and this emphasis on organization may be a happy augury for the future. Nevertheless, there appears to be much stress still on State sovereignty. The Dumbarton Oaks Conversations on World Organization, out of which U.N.O. sprang, laid down as the first of six principles that "the Organization is based on the principle of the sovereign equality of all peace-loving States".[1] This may have been the result of an effort to find a *modus vivendi* and a recognition of things as they exist. As such, it may prove to be the means of overcoming immediate difficulties along the lines of accepted

[1] Cmmd. 6560.

international practice, but it seems that a further step will be necessary before a more satisfactory world order can be set up. What is needed is a supra-national body which will have power to impose agreed lines of conduct in certain cases. The constitution and powers of such an authority are beyond the scope of Political Geography, yet its establishment could have such a tremendous influence on world-wide affairs, that it seems to be the all-important next stage in that evolution of States which has been briefly analysed here.

III

INTERNAL POLITICAL GEOGRAPHY

THE internal and external relationships of modern States are not, in any strict sense, capable of separation. They are too closely interdigitated in a world of increasing economic interdependence to be regarded as distinct elements. The type of economy, the degree of organization and the form of government developed in any one State are certain to affect its relationships with its fellows, both those close at hand and others at greater distances. Yet, for purposes of analysis, it is helpful to examine the politico-geographical conditions of the State from each of the two aspects.

Within its territorial limits, every State possesses a physical background or environment, but no two States are exactly alike in this setting. Largely because of these differences in internal physical conditions, human adaptations vary from State to State. The same general principle of response is discernible everywhere, because mankind is compelled to win the means of survival by utilizing the resources which the environment provides, but once that prerequisite of human life and activity is conceded, the forms and details of the response vary widely. So also there is a great diversity in the levels of organization which different States have reached, both in comparable environments and at different times.

In general, it seems that the higher the level of organization and technical efficiency which is attained in a State, the less effective becomes the deterministic influence of the physical environment, but it must be admitted that not one of the present States has succeeded in eliminating completely the effects of "natural" conditions. This indicates the desirability of attempting an assessment of the more important physical elements in the structure of the State, with the reservation that a particular set of physical conditions will not necessarily produce a given response. Human activities are rarely, if ever, predictable.

34

To many people, Geography consists largely of the answers to the question, "Where is it?", whether in reference to a State or to any other part of the earth's surface. While refusing to accept the validity of this inadequate view, geographers will admit that the locational factor in the study of a State is of great importance, but will also agree that the value of position alters with changing conditions in many ways. In its very early history a State may well derive advantage from isolation, particularly if, during its formative period, it is encircled by protective zones such as the sea or the desert or forests. But sooner or later the surrounding barriers are overcome and contact is established with other parts of the world.

This may lead to danger for the growing State if it is inadequately endowed with resources for self-defence, but it also leads to access to the means of further development. New items are added to its people's diet, previously unobtainable materials become available to its industries, markets for its surplus commodities are extended and new ideas, new skills, become accessible to its inhabitants. In fact, a whole range of material and cultural gains is put in the way of a State once its location with regard to other States is utilized, and that range will extend with the number and intimacy of the contacts as well as with the receptive and reciprocal tendencies of its people and their neighbours. Land contact is not necessary for this purpose, nor indeed is close contiguity. Once the difficulties of sea transport are overcome, all the advantages of immediate contact may be secured, while the disadvantages of being too close to neighbours are avoided.

The best illustration of this type of location is to be found in Great Britain, where insularity and easy access to the Continent of Europe have been exploited with remarkably successful results. Of Europe, but not in it, summarizes this aspect of Britain's location, and if it be asserted that the Narrow Seas would have had no protective influence without the Royal Navy, then the reply is that this branch of Britain's defences is but one result of the people's efforts to adapt their activities to this particular environmental condition.

Again location decides the type or types of climate which are experienced in a State. The argument that all the great modern independent States are either situated in, or have developed their homelands in, the so-called Temperate Zone is a familiar one. On the available evidence, these Temperate Lands, even if they are sometimes far from being "temperate", appear to provide the optimum climatic environment for that aggregation of human activities which is epitomized in the highest forms of political organization.

Too little is known at present concerning the relationships between people and climatic conditions to be dogmatic on this matter. Much reliable scientific data must be collected before any certainty can be expressed on the precise character of optimum climatic conditions for human development, but there remain the undeniable facts that no important States have developed in areas of permanently excessive cold such as the circumpolar regions, and that, so far, no modern independent States have found their location in those parts of the earth where very high average temperatures prevail throughout the year. The former climatic background possesses the more permanent conditioning character, in spite of Russian achievements in the Arctic areas of Eurasia, but recent political developments in the former Netherlands East Indies and in India may be pointers to a reorientation of opinions concerning the retarding influence of continually high temperatures on political growth. The matter will be more fully discussed later; sufficient has been said here to show that the locational value of a State is enhanced through the climatic conditions which a particular situation entails.

Location of a State has another result which affects its Political Geography intimately. In Europe, which contains more independent States than any other area of comparable size, the strategic aspect of location receives a great deal of attention. No one who was familiar with Germany during the interwar years will deny the effects on that country's internal affairs of the fears which were centred on the dangers of "Encirclement". By means of cleverly devised maps and diagrams, by inflammatory speeches and by seemingly endless articles and books, the German people were persuaded into acquiescence in the National Socialist policy of rearmament which had serious results in the country's internal economy.

Again, the French Government was obsessed with the dangers of their country's location face to face with Germany. No Frenchman ever doubted the necessity of compulsory military service—many of them could not understand why conscription for military service was not put into practice in Great Britain—and the proportion of the State revenues devoted to defence purposes was a serious hindrance to the economic progress of that country. At the same time, the defeatism of "Maginot mentality" had disturbing effects on the whole fabric of French life.

Furthermore, French industrial policy has been largely modified by the presence of Germany on her eastern frontier. Witness the growth of industries away from the only large coal resources of the country in Pas de Calais and Le Nord; the development of electro-chemical and electro-metallurgical plants in the French Alps, and particularly the establishment of hydro-electricity generating stations in the Alps, the Pyrenees and in the Massif Central. The mining of iron ore in Normandy, when the largest European reserves of that commodity are available in Lorraine, is another outcome of French fears of German aggression. Even the U.S.S.R., with its vast territory and material resources, feels the impact of the locational factor on its internal organization. The most spectacular example of rapid adjustment to strategic consider-ations is to be seen in the growth of large-scale industrial units in Soviet Asia, that is "behind the Urals", remote from the threat of attack from European sources. It is difficult for the foreign observer to appreciate fully the reality of such fears, but the evidence is available in the trends revealed by the internal policies of many States, a few examples of which are given here.

Closely allied with the locational factor as a geographical element in the internal affairs of the State are considerations of size and shape. Every State has grown to its present size from relatively small beginnings in the form of a nuclear area from which expansion has taken place, and which generally retains a dominant position in the internal organization. France grew out of L'Ile de France, U.S.A. out of the original thirteen colonies on the Atlantic seaboard, the U.S.S.R. out of Muscovy and, to show that the workings of this principle are not confined to modern times, the Roman Empire grew out of a small nucleus in Latium. Size or space inevitably plays a major role in the organization of a State if for no other reason than that its relations with the nuclear area must be facilitated and organized, lest failure to tie together the outlying parts with the centre leaves the former open to the threat of acquisition by rival States. Also, in the great majority of cases, additional territory is desired and sometimes acquired as a means of extending the resources of the State or for strategic reasons. Only in very recent years has the theory of trusteeship, by which an advanced State undertakes the organization of a "backward" region in the interests of its inhabitants, been adumbrated.

Provided that its resources are fully exploited on an organized basis, the very large State has tremendous power at its disposal. Because of the diversity of the earth's surface, any very large territory will contain a variety of environments, each with its own material resources. Within its limits, there will be varied geological structures and rock types, so that minerals are almost certain to be available. Moreover, such a State will embrace a number of climates, important in themselves but of greater value when related to human activities through the associated vegetation types, natural and cultivated, which they make possible. The U.S.S.R. and U.S.A. stand out as examples of this kind of large State, both possessing enormous wealth and power and both strenuously engaged in organizing their endowments. They are alike also in other respects. Each occupies a vast but compact area of the earth. Each is a State of continuous territory on a continental scale, wherein no problems of lack of space or overpopulation are likely to arise for a very long time, and each now possesses access to oceanic outlets, both east and west. Never before have such vast "Empires" of this character been known, and certainly no such actual and potential capacities for production of a great variety of commodities have ever existed within the framework of a continuous land State. Clearly, there is almost unimaginable scope for experimentation in organization, agricultural, industrial, commercial and political, in each of these phenomenal States, and great developments are to be expected in the measurable future. Their present influence in world affairs is an index of the degree to which their internal organization has been already adapted to the problems of space.

That size alone is not always a decisive factor in the greatness of States must be recognized. China, Brazil, Canada and Australia all have very large territories, but in each there are elements which have, so far, restricted internal organization to the extent that not one of these four more or less independent States is considered to be a Great Power. China appears to possess the essential resources of area and population but has not succeeded in utilizing its latent power, largely, it seems, for psychological reasons. Brazil, Canada and Australia all suffer from inadequate population resources over large parts of their territories. The population map of each of these three countries shows that the most densely occupied areas are marginal in location and that large areas are, for climatic reasons, almost uninhabited. Excessive heat, usually accompanied by heavy rainfall and dense forest, in Brazil, excessive cold in Canada and aridity in Australia, explain why these States contain unpopulated and therefore undeveloped areas but it would be unwise to urge that these climatic conditions, which have been deterministic up to the present, will continue to restrict economic and political developments. U.S.A. and U.S.S.R. also contain large areas which are inimical to human settlement and organization, but their more favourable latitudinal extent gives them a greater proportion of territory in which human efforts win greater rewards.

Although the examples of U.S.A. and U.S.S.R. indicate the advantages of continuity of area in a very large State, the territory of some other large political units is discontinuous and, in certain cases, is widely dispersed over the surface of the earth. These are the great Colonial Powers which are not strictly comparable with States in the sense the term has been employed in these pages. The British, French, Dutch, Belgian, and other similar Colonial Empires are States in so far as they are administered by and owe allegiance to a central authority, in which is vested sovereign power but which remains in the "motherland", or "home country", which is a State in its own right. In practice, colonies are regarded as appendages of the mother State. Only by secession, as in the case of the early North American colonies, or by acquiring "Dominion Status", as exemplified in the British Commonwealth, can colonies elevate themselves to the rank of independent States, but in the second of these two procedures there remain certain ties, more particularly in the matter of relationship to the British Throne, and also ties of sentiment. The legal relationship between mother country and colonies, with which dependencies, protectorates and mandated territories may be included for present purposes, varies in the different Colonial Empires, but with the possible exception of Algeria, which is officially a part of Metropolitan France, there is no question of equality between the components of such Empires.

Nevertheless, the possession of colonial territories, especially when they are widely spread but in the aggregate form large areas, has important effects on the internal affairs of the mother State. Not only do they provide careers for administrators, and markets and materials for merchants and manufacturers, they also make necessary the maintenance of communications and the provision of defensive forces which often result in a heavy drain on the revenue of the possessing Power.

One final remark on the possible effects of size may be permissible here. Great size in a State, whether the whole territory is equally valuable or not, carries a large amount of prestige for its inhabitants. This is as true of the Colonial Powers as for those not owning colonies. The desire for such prestige, among other things, has driven States to expand, even when little material gain is to be won. Italian acquisition of Eritrea and Libya was an example where overseas expansion was carried out with little benefit to Italy apart from its prestige value, and resulted in a great cost in men and money to the Italian people. It seems that the very fact of extending power over increasing area gives a feeling of satisfaction and of achievement to successfully expanding peoples, and in certain cases has had a stimulating effect on at least some of the State's internal relations. Just how far the prestige factor has been beneficial or detrimental to the internal organization of the State it is very difficult to judge, but that it has acted as a motivating force in the growth of States can hardly be denied.

Whatever the location and size of a State, its territory possesses physical characteristics which the political geographer cannot afford to ignore because, apart from the State's external relationships, this physical basis is the source of the material sustenance of its inhabitants and there must be, therefore, close relations between land and people. Furthermore, those relationships are not susceptible to complete analysis unless and until the contributions of each of these elements in the State are recognized, but in examining the physical background there is less danger of falling into error than in a similar survey of the human contribution. The actual land on which a State develops changes at a much slower rate than that which characterizes human changes, especially at the organizational level. It is also more tangible, less imponderable, than the other element and therefore lends itself more readily to investigation.

At the outset it should be pointed out that any given physical framework, whether of a State or not, is always the result of a combination of factors which are often treated separately for the sake of convenience, but which, in fact, combine in a variety of ways to produce a surface area which becomes the territorial fabric of a State or States. Thus the land forms derived from geological structure, itself the result of the events of geological history, are modified by climatic conditions through subaerial erosional activities to produce, here, one type of physical environment and there another.

Again, rivers are in part a function of the climate or climates of a region, but are closely influenced as to volume, rate and direction of flow by the rock types which they cross, and the occurrence of which depends on a number of geological factors. Clearly, the detailed study of land-forms, including their causation, lies outside the scope of Political Geography, but knowledge of their nature is helpful in assessing the part they play in the internal relationships of the State, just as it is to the worker in the wider field of Human Geography.

Geological structure merits a place in the study of the

Political Geography of a State for two reasons. In the first place, the State's mineral resources are a direct result of its geological structure, and there is no need to emphasize the importance of accessible mineral resources in these days when large-scale industry, which is largely dependent on minerals in one form or another, is the main pillar of the State's power.

Furthermore, geological structure is responsible for the distribution and degree of accessibility of minerals as well as for their presence or absence. It is difficult to overstress the importance of this factor, for example, in the internal Political Geography of Great Britain. In this particular State the Industrial Revolution was facilitated by the close contiguity of accessible supplies of coal, iron ore, and other minerals. Even allowing for the inventive genius of some of its people, it is difficult to see how the application of steam-power and the uses of iron and steel to industrial processes could have been brought about in the absence of such basic materials, and no one will deny that industrialization has revolutionized the internal affairs of Britain. In point of fact, the growth of industries has been a major factor in the development of the internal relationships of all the great modern States, and more particularly so since their industrial productivity became a decisive factor in warfare.

The second reason for the relevance of geological structure in Political Geography is that it determines the major lineaments of the surface of a State. These relief features, modified as they may be by forces other than those directly associated with structure, play an important part in human activities. Plains, particularly when they have a coastal location, have provided the corelands of many States, but mountainous areas often possess great resources in timber, minerals and water-power, which human ingenuity has succeeded in utilizing to expand the economic and political power of the State. Again, where a mountainous State lies between areas of dense population and great economic productivity, its internal resources may be strengthened by the control of routeways linking the separated areas, as the case of Switzerland shows.

In general, political unification is more easily achieved in areas of plains than on mountainous terrain. Large parts of truly mountainous country are uninhabited; people are confined to valleys so that population is unevenly spread in scattered groups between which communication is not easily made, so that the social unit tends to be the clan, and may give rise to a territorial organization such as the canton. Only in an advanced stage of political evolution are these distinct units brought together in one State. On the other hand, movement and contact between the inhabitants of larger areas are more easily developed on plains so that trade and the diffusion of ideas are facilitated to a greater extent than among mountains. But those very facilities which encourage the development of States on plains also encourage the expansion of adjacent States, and lead to rivalry. Greater effort is therefore necessary to maintain the territorial integrity of States which consist mainly of plains. The ease with which expansion of a powerful State can take place on such terrain explains why each of the world's great plains has either been incorporated in one State or has become a region of competition between rival States.

Examples of the former case are to be seen in the inclusion of the Siberian Plains in the U.S.S.R., and the Middle West in U.S.A. The European Plain provides the clearest example of the locus of an age-old conflict between rival groups, the result of which is clearly reflected in the present pattern of States. In each of the political units of that battleground there remains the fear of encroachment by neighbour States with all the repercussions on its internal organization. Conversely, mountainous terrain often provides facilities for refuge, and not only against territorial expansion, or it may exert a protective influence behind which a State may achieve political security although it suffers from economic and cultural isolation.

In the past, and to a less extent today, rivers have played a dual role both in the evolution of States and in their internal activities. In these apparently contradictory functions the character of the riparian areas has also been important. The value of a river in its significance to a State or States depends partly on the nature of the valley it occupies but also on the physical conditions of the land immediately adjacent to its banks. Before man was able to bridge rivers and to drain the riverine areas, rivers were often accepted as State boundaries, partly because they were easily identifiable and relatively permanent features in the landscape, but more often because they, together with their marshy flood plains, were ready-made defensive zones. In this sense, rivers fulfilled a separating function, but not necessarily along their entire lengths, as the use of parts of the Rhine and Danube in the boundary system of the Roman Empire illustrates.

Even in the earliest States, and certainly in modern cases, rivers have more often been unifying factors. They or their valleys usually provide the easiest lines of human movement, even on plains, so that circulation in a State, which is an essential component in its internal organization, tends to follow river lines more particularly before railways were introduced. When the latter became a well-nigh universal means of transport, their constructors utilized the easier gradients which valleys afford and thus re-emphasized the unifying influence of rivers, since they, in conjunction with geological structure, are responsible for the valley types and patterns. In regions of permanent or seasonal aridity rivers may be the very lifeblood of a State and leave an indelible mark on its organization. Modern Egypt, like its ancient predecessor, and Iraq are largely dependent on the waters of the Nile and the Tigris-Euphrates respectively for the irrigation of crops; they might almost be called irrigation States. Elsewhere the use of river water for irrigation purposes is not such a dominant factor in the life of the State, but the Indus and Ganges in India, the Hwang-ho in China, are outstanding examples of the ways in which rivers contribute to the State's effective resources, while many smaller-scale examples may be cited in all the continents.

Since the opening of the twentieth century rivers have assumed another function in the human activities of the State. For a very long time they have been a source of mechanical energy, but it was only with the discovery of the use of running water as a means of generating electricity that rivers could compete with oil and coal as suppliers of both industrial power and illumination. As the capacity of a river for this purpose depends on its volume and rate of flow, its power potential may be regarded as a function of relief and climate combined. Hence States which contain mountain areas with a heavy precipitation are well endowed in this connection, and that endowment is all the more important when coal and oil are absent. Switzerland, Sweden and Norway provide excellent examples of States which, poor in other sources of energy, have been able to overcome difficulties inherent in their physical environment by utilizing their rivers for the generation of hydro-electricity.

Rivers, as highways, as sources of electrical energy, as suppliers of water for irrigation economies, are clearly an important element in the internal Political Geography of States, and the struggle for control of them for one or more of these purposes frequently leads to strife between neighbouring Riparian Powers so that the external relationships are also affected by interests in river control. Some riverine States consider it essential to extend their sovereignty over the mouths of the rivers which flow through their territory, claiming that their internal development is dependent on full access to the sea by this means.

This raises the question of another element in the physical background of the State, that is, the possession and utilization of seaboards. The economic interdependence of the various parts of the earth's surface, which has been stressed in an earlier chapter, is largely the outcome of the growth, speed and relative cheapness of ocean transport by which the great majority of world circulation is maintained. In order to share fully in this world trade, and therefore to be able to develop its internal economy, it is considered highly desirable for a State to possess a seaboard so that it may maintain its own merchant marine. From this point of view, a location in the interior of a continent is obviously a disadvantage, and efforts have been made to overcome it, as in the case of Czecho-slovakia's former Free Zone at Hamburg.

Granted that a State is unable to develop fully without access to world markets and supplies of commodities, the value of a seaboard is apparent, but varies according to location of the coast and its character. In this regard the northern shores of Canada and the U.S.S.R. are so far of little importance, but those coasts which face on to the world's great ocean highways are of great value. France, with a seaboard on the Atlantic and on the Mediterranean, has known how to utilize this double advantage to her internal organization, while Anglo-German rivalry has resulted in the support given to Belgium and Holland by England, to prevent Germany from expanding to the North Sea on a front larger than that she already possesses. Some measure of the importance attached to this coastal factor is the generally accepted principle of the extension of the State's sovereignty to a distance of three or more miles out to sea, but, within certain limits, the physical character of the State's seaboard has lost some of its original value. Provided that the coast gives access to ocean highways and to the interior of the State concerned, man's engineering skill is such that harbours can be built where natural facilities are not greatly favourable to dock construction.

Nevertheless, it remains true that the world's great ports have been developed in physically favourable situations, but the dominant factor has been two-way accessibility, to the seas and to the interior. Lastly, it is worth noting that accessibility to the sea through the possession of a seaboard leads, in some cases, to the growth of a fishing industry which may play an important part in the State's internal life. In this sense, adjacent or even remote fishing-grounds may be regarded as a territorial extension of the State, in so far as they provide additional resources, not only in the supply of foodstuffs and articles of trade, but as a source of recruitment for naval purposes.

The relationship between climatic conditions and human activity has already been mentioned in another context (see pp. 35–36) and the need for a systematic scientific investigation in this field has been stressed. Without underestimating the work of such investigators as Ellsworth Huntington and Griffith Taylor, it may be fairly stated that this branch of geographical study is still in the pioneer stage, and much valuable knowledge is likely to accrue from its further progress, not least from the micro-climatological researches which are being conducted in an increasing number of areas. Even so, there can be little doubt that climate is one of the most important elements in the physical environment of the State. While not admitting the closeness of its control of human activities suggested by a recent statement by an American newspaperman,[1] geographers agree that climatic conditions evoke a high degree of adaptation on the part of human beings. They are becoming increasingly aware that deviations from climatic means are often more important than the generalizations which average figures suggest. "Le climat," wrote Vidal de la Blache,"[2] est une résultante qui oscille autour d'une moyenne, plutôt qu'il ne s'y tient."

This fluctuation, frequently of no great amplitude, calls forth even finer adjustments of human activities than do the broad characteristic climatic conditions of a State. Only the smallest of States experience climatic uniformity throughout their territories, whereas the great majority include various climatic types. Even in a small State such as the United Kingdom there is sufficient climatic differentiation to give rise to diversity in human habitats. Most potent to man of all the influences of climate is that exerted through vegetation on agricultural occupations. In their natural state, plants are more susceptible to climatic control than to any other single element, and, although human achievements in cultivating and developing plants are remarkable for the amount of ingenuity shown, it nevertheless remains true that agriculture is still largely dependent on climate. The great circumpolar regions, with their fringes of Tundra in the Northern Hemisphere, and the great deserts, together comprising a large proportion of the earth's surface, are still not habitable, and for climatic reasons. In the so-called Temperate Lands, the types of agriculture are broadly determined by climatic conditions.

Both the production of foodstuffs and of vegetable raw materials for other purposes than human consumption are closely associated with conditions of temperature, rainfall and so forth, not only in their totality, but also in their seasonal

[1] "In South Dakota, the average rainfall is eighteen inches a year. When it drops to sixteen everybody goes broke. When it hits nineteen the farmers light cigars with 100-dollar bills." (P. Gallico, American Correspondent of the *Sunday Graphic*, November 3rd, 1946.)

[2] P. Vidal de la Blache, *Principes de Géographie Humaine*, Paris, 1921, p.14.

incidence. Now maintenance of an adequate food supply is an essential objective of the internal organization of a State, therefore, given sufficient space in relation to its population, a State which is endowed with a variety of climates, even if the variation is of no great range, should be able to provide sufficient food for its people and, what is becoming more generally appreciated, a balanced diet. Under these favourable climatic conditions the potential energy output of its inhabitants is higher than in less favoured countries. This means that climatic conditions are of primary importance in the Political Geography of States, since their political power rests largely on the production output of their people.

Again, if the State is not in possession of adequate space for food production purposes under existing agricultural systems it must either import the necessary commodities or it must intensify its own production. Intensification and expansion of crop cultivation are closely related to climate. Few States, for example, can regularly produce more than one crop per year without highly artificial, and therefore costly, assistance. This is particularly true of those countries with long rigorous winters when plant life is reduced to a standstill, and densely populated States, such as the United Kingdom, which enjoy more genial winter conditions, have been able to increase their home production only by such means as subsidies and protective measures, which affect not only their internal organization but also their external relationships.

On the other hand, climatic complexity working through its effects on agricultural activities can be an adverse factor, especially in those large States which embrace several distinctive climatic types. In U.S.A., the farming communities of the Middle West are frequently at variance with the Federal Government in Washington, asserting that the administration there is unfamiliar with the problems of agriculture and crop marketing which are the predominant interests of the Middle Westerners. Similarly in Canada, the chief complaint of the farmers of the Prairie Provinces appears to be that the Ottawa Government pays insufficient attention to their interests. These internal disputes are no doubt associated with the great distances between the administrative capital and the recalcitrant regions, but the basic conflict is one between different economies related to differences in climate.

At times of exacerbation, such quarrels constitute a threat to the political and economic unity of the State; in the cases of the two Dominions of Canada and Australia, Alberta and W. Australia have gone so far as to suggest secession. These, and other examples, suggest that where there is a wide range of climatic conditions they and their agricultural results must be considered if the State is to run smoothly. In brief, no State can afford to ignore the influences of the climatic element in its physical environment, and a wise administration will seek to organize the utilization of its climatic resources to the maximum benefit of its inhabitants.

In the preceding pages of this chapter, the closely related elements of the physical framework of States have been all too incompletely analysed, but these conditions are meaningless to the political geographer, apart from the people who organize their activities and relationships in adjustment to them and within the territorial limits of political entities. This human element in the State is even more complex than the physical elements of the *milieu* which it inhabits. Diversity is still the keynote in the human response to environment in spite of "cultural spread", facilitated by greatly improved means of communications. No State can justly claim to have a completely homogeneous human content. The only uniformity which it possesses is that arising from its political organization by which, in theory at least, its members owe allegiance to the sovereignty it wields. Even in this last connection it is worth recalling that, over vast portions of the earth's surface, as in Central Africa, in India, in China, and in parts of South America, political allegiance is but a tenuous thing and the internal human relationships of States should not always be measured by the standards reached in Western Europe and North America.

Total population, its distributional pattern and rates of reproduction, are essential elements in the structure of the State. Without quantitative knowledge, such as that which regularly taken censuses provide, the organization of internal activities is greatly impeded. This does not mean that mere size of population is the final determinant of the greatness of States. Quality must also be considered, but the fact remains that a State with insufficient manpower to utilize its resources is unable to maintain desirable standards of living, and is unlikely to bring about the smooth running of its internal affairs. There can be no doubt that the application of mechanical processes in industry, agriculture and commerce has greatly increased the output per man hour, and has also helped to reduce the necessary hours of employment in the more advanced countries, yet the human element is still of vital importance, and it is unlikely that foreseeable developments will change the validity of this claim. The demographic structure of the State is therefore of fundamental significance to the political geographer, whether he is immediately concerned with internal or external relationships. (See Chapter VII.)

The quality of this human content rests on the combined effects of a number of factors, each of which makes its contribution, but in varying degree according to the particular circumstances which exist at any given time. Change in territorial extent, in size of population or in the system of government gives rise to modifications of the influence of these factors. The present form and content of a State represent a stage in its evolution so that historical elements play an important role in its present organization. In no case can the history and associated accomplishments of a State be erased. Experience gained in the past is used, directly or indirectly, as guidance in the present. Too much tradition and too many precedents may act as barriers to progress, but in a well-balanced State they receive their due share of consideration. The educative function of a steady evolution, uninterrupted by abrupt changes, is of inestimable advantage to the development of good internal relations. "Revolution by evolution" means that the people of a State are enabled to adapt their activities to changing conditions without major acts of violence.

Secondly, the ethnic structure of the State must be considered as a human factor in its internal Political Geography. Here the student is confronted with a mass of difficulties and problems which may appear insuperable, and the analysis of which requires much more space than is available in this book.

Nevertheless, certain facts are clear. No State possesses a homogeneous ethnic structure, and racial purity, in the correct biological sense, is non-existent. Persistent and widely spread migrations together with continual intermarriage have resulted in such a mixture of peoples that, although ethnologists suggest various broad groupings on the basis of certain physical characteristics, there is no possibility of defining these groups by acceptable linear boundaries. But the State, by its nature, must be clearly defined, i.e. the territory over which it exercises sovereign power must be delimited precisely and accurately. In the result, States must include areas inhabited by people of different ethnic origins; hence all States are ethnically heterogeneous.

Europe is particularly affected in this way, partly because of its close contacts with Asia whence many immigrants have come over a long period of history, and partly because it is the most complexly fragmented of all the continents. At the same time, the Americas, Monsoon Asia and Africa all have their ethnic problems. Given good will and reasonableness, ethnic differences should not hinder the internal unity of a State, but it appears that in most cases these desirable qualities are lacking, since a welter of myths and ideologies, epitomized in the term "race-consciousness", has been built up and now provides a formidable barrier to the successful integration of the human elements. Prejudice and differential treatment arising out of ethnic differences are inimical to good administration. Where ethnic minorities and enclaves exist and are deprived of equality of status, they are sources of weakness and friction in the State structure. In some cases, as in the former Austro-Hungarian Empire, they may lead to dissolution.

While there is some relationship between present ethnic groups and their racial origins in the remote past, the physical characteristics which mark races are no longer applicable as differentiating factors in the determination of ethnic distributions, hence some other distinguishing feature is sought and is usually found in language. In general, this course is justifiable as the possession and use of a common language are the most easily recognizable evidence of a common ethnic origin and of a common culture. Indeed, the extent to which ethnic groups persist in retaining their language is remarkable. After centuries of domination by Austria, the Slovenes of Jugoslavia retained their language, although it was not recognized by their conquerors. The evidence suggests that it is impossible to eliminate a language by force or other means, except, perhaps, by slow decay, and the importance attached to language as an element in the State's structure is illustrated by efforts to revive it, as in Eire. Since States are ethnically heterogeneous and since ethnic groups show the marked feature of language retention, it follows that very few States are unilingual. This lack of linguistic unity may be another factor opposed to the solidarity and oneness of the State, more particularly when language difficulties represent ethnical and cultural diversity in an active form.

Apart from the regrettable uses made of linguistic differences for unjustifiable political purposes, such as the propagation of unsound ideologies, the role of language in the internal Political Geography of States depends on its function as the medium of social intercourse. Language is the vehicle of thought and, as Rundle[1] shows, the use of a particular language tends to impose certain restrictions on the capacity for thought and thought development. Furthermore, "speakers of different languages possess somewhat different mental make-up, and their thought processes do not run along exactly the same lines".[2] Hence in a State where all the people, or even a great majority, speak the same language, unity is likely to be more easily achieved, and the internal relationships will therefore be liable to closer integration. Conversely, where more than one tongue is in common use, barriers to intercourse will occur and greater difficulty is experienced in organizing State activities.

This explains why the use of the "official" language was imposed on conquered or annexed territories, at least for State purposes, such as those connected with the law, administration and so forth, but, in spite of these efforts, the use of different languages fosters a stratification of society into linguistic "layers", each of which is divorced from full association with its fellows even though they may be equal in law. Here lies an obvious weakness in the structure of the multilingual State and one which cannot be rectified by the imposition of one selected language. The solution lies in "freedom of speech", and the development of bi-lingualism rather than in the forced acceptance of a monotonous linguistic uniformity.

Religion, or more accurately, adherence to an organized Church, is another human element which has a bearing on the internal Political Geography of States. Maturely developed States usually practise toleration in religious matters and, in consequence, differences in creed exercise little effect on their organization, but less advanced States may be influenced in one of two ways. Where the majority of people adhere to a common faith, such a belief exerts a powerful unifying force in so far as the shared experiences of its members give rise to a feeling of "belonging together", which may be carried over to more mundane affairs. Even so, areas occupied by religious groups, i.e. of people belonging to one faith, are never exactly coincident with the territory of a single State. All the great religions of the world were propagated before States assumed their present forms, before their boundaries were clearly defined and demarcated, so that it is not uncommon to find adherence to more than one religion within a State and, where toleration is not practised, such differences may give rise to internal conflict and to external dissension.

It is no part of the political geographer's task to assess the merits or the demerits of religious beliefs, but he is forced to recognize that this human element is as disruptive in some cases as it is unifying in others. Whereas in the Jugoslav State the clash between Roman Catholicism and the Serbian Orthodox Church has engendered divergence in outlook as between Slovenes and Croats on the one hand and Serbs on the other, the Polish people have been drawn together by the widespread membership of the Roman Catholic Church in their country. Again, the apparent inability of the great religious groups of India to work together is proving to be one of the most serious obstacles to the achievement of political unity in that sub-continental area.

All these elements in the human content of a State give colour and variety, diversity and complexity, to its body politic. Historical background, numbers and densities of population, ethnic origins and associated cultural traditions, language and religion, all contribute their share to the variegated pattern which every State, great or small, exhibits, and a sound test of its degree of maturity may be found in the extent to which these elements are constructively utilized to further the material and spiritual welfare of its inhabitants. All the evidence, from the past and the present, goes to suggest that persecution and repression are inimical to human welfare, whereas tolerance and even encouragement of sectional interests enrich the life of the State, give it greater virility, and make possible that pursuit of happiness which may be con-sidered as the ultimate objective. But these social and ethical considerations are not the primary concern of the political geographer. His field of study lies in the relationships between these human elements and their physical environment with special reference to their spatial distribution, and in investi-gating these internal relationships he is confronted with a paradox which is evident in each and every State.

It has already been emphasized that the hallmark of the State is its sovereign power with the corollary of allegiance by its inhabitants. In practice, that sovereignty is exercised by a central Government, in some form or other, which gathers to itself greater powers with the passage of time and with the development of organization. Without some central authority, responsible for general policy in social, economic and political affairs, the State cannot provide the optimum conditions for the satisfying adaptation of its people's activities to their physical background. This was true enough in the days of *laissez faire* economics, but carries greater weight in those States which are endeavouring to evolve planned economies, and is carried to extreme lengths in totalitarian States.

The conclusion is inescapable. The growth of organization is coincidental with an increase in the centralization of power, until the central authority becomes so overloaded with the tasks of administration that there is serious danger of breakdown in the State machinery. This is particularly true of States today, because of the great complexity of administration and of the increasing amplitude of the problems which administrators are called upon to handle. Members of a central Government cannot be expected to be sufficiently familiar with all the requirements of the different parts of the State, especially where that territory is large, hence the growth of the practice of delegating power to "local authorities", through legislation of either compulsory or permissive character.

These local authorities vary widely in the power they possess, in the areas they administer and according to the structure of the State of which they form parts. Nevertheless, they tend to acquire increasing power as the State becomes more highly organized, and therefore give rise to the paradoxical situation in which centralization increases with the evolution of the State and at the same time makes necessary a degree of devolution. This parallelism is apparent in all modern states, but the administrative pattern which results from it varies greatly. In the great Federal States of the world, for example in U.S.A., Canada and Australia, the administrative states or provinces have considerable autonomy, but in smaller, more compact States, such as the majority of those in Europe, the internal divisions, counties, *départements*, etc., are not autonomous but have considerable administrative authority within the general framework.

In some cases the internal divisions represent the summation of regional affiliations over a long period of time; in others, they have been imposed by the central Government mainly for ease of administration and bear little relation to the social, economic and historical backgrounds of their inhabitants. But with the replacement of *laissez faire* by a system based on planned economy it is becoming ever more necessary to devise a pattern of internal divisions which will not only be more appropriate to the requirements of the State as a whole, but will give greater facilities for the co-ordination and planning of regional human activities than have hitherto been available. This is no easy task. The whole machinery of government is based on the existence of clearly defined areas, and changes in their boundaries lead to anomalies and difficulties, not the least of which, from the geographer's point of view, is that where boundary changes take place it becomes very difficult to make statistical comparisons over any considerable length of time.

A more serious weakness is found in most States because the internal divisions were made to conform to conditions in a more or less remote past and sufficient adjustment to changed conditions has not been made. The most serious weakness, however, is that administrative needs, at least in so far as delimitation of boundaries is concerned, are regarded as an end in themselves rather than as a means to the end of regional unification and "wholeness". That is one reason why so many regional divisions of Great Britain have been suggested or applied.[1] That realization of the anachronistic character of the older administrative divisions is spreading is suggested by recent changes in U.S.S.R., Germany and Jugoslavia as well as by the growth of a strong "Regionalist" movement in France. Once it is appreciated that regionalism need not lessen the unifying power at the centre but that it can be a creative force, both in the co-ordination of human activities within the region and in the integration of regional affairs inside the State, then the effort to overcome the difficulties associated with changes of the existing administrative boundaries will be seen to be worth while.

[1] *Cf.* the series of 25 maps illustrating "Practical Regionalism in England and Wales", by E. W. Gilbert, *Geographical Journal*, London, Vol. xciv, July 1939.

IV

INTER–STATE RELATIONSHIPS

THE internal and external relationships of States are complementary to each other. Although they are discussed in separate chapters in this book for the purposes of analysis and description, they are not separable in practice. They grow and develop side by side and simultaneously, and the more they can be kept in step with each other, the more benefits are likely to be conferred on the inhabitants of the various countries. Indeed, it is no exaggeration to claim that the achievement of harmony between the internal and external relationships of all States is a necessary prerequisite to the development of human well-being in the world as a whole.

Two factors illustrate this point clearly. One is the ever-increasing economic interdependence of States, never more clearly evidenced than in the present position of world-wide shortages in the great majority of commodities. The second is the gradual breaking down of barriers between the States with the growth and spread of knowledge through the rapid expansion of means of communication. In the latter case, the two world wars of the twentieth century have undoubtedly played a part if only because millions of men and women have travelled beyond the confines of their homelands and, at the very least, have become aware of the existence of other peoples.

Add to this the knowledge that strategic considerations have been modified by the changes brought about in modern warfare, and it is not difficult to appreciate the fact that the external relationships of States are no longer the entire responsibility of a handful of statesmen, but are intimately and directly the concern of all citizens of all States. In this sense it is legitimate to speak of a slowly emerging world opinion, as yet unformed and in many ways inhibited by fears and suspicions based on past activities, but capable of exerting pressure on world affairs and already equipped with platforms and mouthpieces in the various international organizations which have been established.

Given these premises, the political geographer may well ask for a definition of the sphere of his studies in this maze of difficult and often intractable problems which is usually known as international affairs. The first answer to this question is that there can be no hard and fast line marking off the purely geographical aspects of inter-State relationships from all other aspects. To think of the relationships between States as confined in watertight compartments would be to deny all the evidence provided by intelligent observation and deduction. Indeed, these relationships, together with their problems and disputes, like all human relationships, have a composite character in which many factors are blended to such an extent that they are incapable of clear separation.

Nevertheless, the foreign policy of a State is usually dominated by one or more aspects of its relations with other States. The Soviet Union, for example, appears to be obsessed with the desire for military security, behind which it hopes to achieve economic and social reconstruction in line with its particular political theories. Again, the foreign relations of France, as well as its internal affairs, are still largely dominated by fear of possible German aggression.

On the other hand, the countries of the Far East, including India, China and Indonesia, are still concerned with further-ing their independence from the political and economic dominance of non-Asian Powers and with a pronounced growth of nationalist tendencies, and their external relation-ships are accordingly biased by these considerations. These, and many other examples, may be put forward as illustrations of the complexity and diversity of the foreign relationships of States, and they indicate that, while there is no clear line of demarcation, many of the ingredients of external relations are beyond the scope of geographical investigation.

Having admitted this limitation of Political Geography in this particular field of study, it is now possible to give the second and more important answer to the question put above. Whatever form the global pattern of States may assume, and whatever stage the inter-State relations may reach, the fact remains that each State must occupy territory, and the activities of its inhabitants must be more or less conditioned by the physical characteristics of that territory.

This physical environment of the State is only part of a greater, world, background in which considerations of space, distance and location play a vital part, not only in matters of military strategy but also in agricultural and industrial production as well as in the distribution of all kinds of commodities. Hence there exists what may be called a planetary physical environment which provides a framework for inter-State activities in the same way, but on a much larger scale, as the physical background of an individual State sets the stage for the internal activities of that organization.

Thus the field of study which the political geographer rightly claims in this connection is the relationship between the external activities of States and the planetary physical stage in which they are set. At the same time, he is compelled to recognize and acknowledge one fundamental distinction between internal and external activities. In the case of the former, the State exerts its sovereign power, sets the pace and guides the activities of its inhabitants; in the latter case, no such overriding power exists. There is, as yet, no world authority which can direct and integrate inter-State affairs. In fact, the great political problem of our times is to find a way of reconciling the necessity for concerted action on the part of all, or even some, States with the exercise of sovereignty in each and every State. Again, it may be argued that this is no concern of the geographer. In that case, the reply must be that the exercise of sovereign power has so frequently modified both internal and external policies that the geographer must take cognizance of its effects if he is to arrive at that balanced view of human activities which should be his objective.

The aspect of inter-State relationships with which Political Geography is primarily concerned, then, is that which arises out of the relation between physical conditions and human activities on a global scale and which find expression in the foreign policies of the constituent States. These relationships fall into a global pattern which is susceptible to change, but which reveals underlying conditions which are worthy of analysis. The late Sir Halford Mackinder was among the first of geographers to postulate such a world pattern. He stressed the need of recognizing "geographical realities", and concluded that "the unequal growth of nations" is the cause, directly or indirectly, of the great wars of history and is "in large measure . . . the result of the uneven distribution of fertility and strategical opportunity upon the face of our Globe".[1]

More recently, Professor Fawcett[2] has re-examined the views of Mackinder and shows that the latter was right when he asserted that "Who rules East Europe commands the Heartland", but that Mackinder's second famous dictum, "Who rules the Heartland commands the World Island", is "much less certain",[3] because the interior of the Old World is at present inadequately populated and insufficiently developed to provide the man-power and material resources with which to overcome the more densely populated marginal lands. Finally Professor Fawcett concludes:

"But, if the Interior power were to extend its rule over the rest of Europe, then the combination of Europe and the Heartland, i.e. an extension to the widest strategic Heartland, would give resources sufficient to *command* the other marginal regions of Mainland, and so to rule the World Island."[4]

The validity of this concept of a world pattern is beyond dispute, and the contrast between interior and marginal lands may become more marked when the Soviet Union has had time to recover from the effects of war. The present alignment of the major States also seems to reflect this geographical pattern. The British Commonwealth and Empire, the U.S.A. and France, all of which fit into Mackinder's scheme of marginal Powers, are clearly united in opposition to Soviet Russia as far as world affairs are concerned. Considered strategically, the Soviet Union possesses many advantages in this arrangement: internal lines of communication, compact and con-

---

[1] H. Mackinder, *op. cit.*, p. 11.
[2] C. B. Fawcett, "The Herbertson Memorial Lecture", published in *Geography*, Vol. xxxii, March 1947.
[3] *Ibid.*, p. 10.
[4] *Ibid.*, p. 11.

tinuous territory, tremendous actual and potential resources and a more or less unified political system. The States which fringe this great Heartland are far from being united politically, and their unity in action, in peace or in war, is hindered also by the fact that their lines of communication are circumferential in relation to the Heartland. Because of world disposition of land and sea masses, these routeways are seaways, the most important of which use the North Atlantic, the Mediterranean, the Red Sea and the Indian Ocean.

In a peaceful world, these blue water links are of great advantage to the States which they serve because sea transport is still the cheapest and most easily maintained for the movement of large quantities of the commodities of commerce, and therefore inter-State relationships are closely connected with their freedom of use. But because of their geographical character, especially in the case of the Mediterranean–Red Sea route which narrows frequently, they are liable to interference. Hence the threat of severance necessitates the maintenance of defensive forces in regions of potential danger, bases must be built and garrisoned, and large scale capital expenditure is required which may have serious repercussions on the internal fiscal policies of individual States.

The situation is well illustrated by the fact that Russia has never been a great naval power, whereas, in the recent past, the United Kingdom, the U.S.A., France, Germany and Japan, all marginal powers in the sense in which the term is used here, have built and maintained great fleets of warships. Britain, in particular, has for over a hundred years placed faith in the Royal Navy as a means of keeping open these all-important seaways. In so doing and in spending vast sums on capital equipment, this outstanding oceanic State has succeeded in fostering the idea of the Freedom of the Seas, to the benefit of its own citizens but equally certainly to the advantage of all those other States whose interests are served by the maintenance of sea-borne trade. In thus undertaking world-wide responsibilities and commitments, Britain has gained great prestige in addition to economic advantages, to the envy of other States which have therefore sought to emulate her example, thus giving rise to rivalry and potential conflict which were only temporarily held in check by agreements on the limitations of naval armaments.

Whereas, therefore, the global pattern suggests the existence of a community of economic interests between the marginal States, even though they show different levels of economic and cultural development, their earlier relationships revealed a failure to recognize this fundamental "geographical reality". Certainly there was no evidence of a conscious joint effort to exploit the facilities provided by the factors of world position, availability of waterways and diversity of resources, with a view to the furtherance of the interests of these marginal lands as a whole. This weakness has been largely eradicated by the creation of the North Atlantic Treaty Organization which represents a deliberate political effort to bring about the unity of what are, in other respects, fourteen disparate political entities.

The external relationships of the Soviet Union have, from its inception, been characterized by an appreciation of the reality of its geographical position in the world pattern. With the single exception of its participation in the Second World War, which, it may be pointed out, was thrust upon it by the German invasion of 1941, the Russian administration has consistently sought to develop its internal economy while safeguarding its contacts with the peripheral powers. By means of territorial acquisition, as in the cases of Lithuania, Latvia, Esthonia and at the expense of Finland, Poland and Roumania, or through the powerful political and economic support given to States such as Poland, Czechoslovakia and Bulgaria, it has succeeded in strengthening its importance as a world Power. For the first time in its history, Russia has something more than "a window on the Baltic". It is unlikely that she will gain a more favourable position in regard to the Straits from a revision of the Montreux Convention, and relations between the Union, on the one hand, and Turkey and Iran on the other, suggest that there has been a deterioration in the Russian strategic position in those countries. Nevertheless, on its western and south-western flanks, the U.S.S.R. has either extended its sovereignty or has developed "spheres of interest" to an extent greater than ever before.

The general situation is no less favourable to Russia on the eastern and southern margins of the Heartland. First and foremost, the emergence of Communist China and the collapse of Japan have removed a serious threat to Soviet security. Secondly, and possibly of greater importance on a long view, is the change in relationships between parts of South-East Asia and West European Powers. India has ceased to be controlled from London, Indonesia has acquired political independence, and the French colonies of South-East Asia have changed their status. It remains to be seen whether the economic ties between the imperial powers of Western Europe and their former dependencies in South-East Asia will be weakened or strengthened by these changes, but the growth towards political independence in the latter areas is favourable to Russian Foreign Policy.

The greater the unity, economic, political, military and cultural, between the marginal lands, the more potential danger there is, in Russian eyes, to the security of the Heartland. But disunity, and the geographical disposition of these lands favours disunity, is advantageous to the Russians because it carries in its train less possibility of concerted action against Soviet policy. That this foreign policy is motivated by a realization of this new alignment of its neighbouring States can hardly be doubted and explains the powerful position which the representatives of the Soviet Union occupy at the tables of the various world conferences.

This elementary analysis of the geographical framework of international affairs should not be read as evidence of the inevitability of conflict, political or military, between the great Heartland State and its neighbours. The U.S.S.R. has by no means achieved a state of invulnerability to attack and partial destruction. Its internal economy is far from being adequately developed and the second world war has destroyed many of the achievements of the preceding twenty-four years of intensive effort. Perhaps more important than this is that relatively little has yet been done to exploit its greatest single geographical advantage, namely its internal lines of communication. In the absence of east-west waterways and in view of the fact that the aeroplane is not yet a suitable means of transport for the large-scale movement of heavy goods and commodities, the European and Asiatic parts of the Union cannot be regarded as enjoying adequate communications.

Furthermore, the high rate of urbanization of the Russian population renders the Union more vulnerable to air attack than ever before. Hence it would be mere fatalism to interpret the global pattern of States as a prelude to yet another world war. Rather does it suggest a framework within which peaceful enjoyment of the fruits of the earth may be brought about. In spite of its vast bulk, in spite of its great resources and even greater potential wealth, the U.S.S.R. and its inhabitants can achieve a higher standard of living by close co-operation, commercially and culturally, with its neighbours.

The task of developing such positive and constructive relations must fall on the responsible statesmen; the political geographer can only indicate, by analysis and description, the geographical framework into which these inter-relationships must fit. The existence of this framework suggests the possibility of a future world unity; the scaffolding and structural skeleton of this global edifice are already available. Yet after a quarter of a century of the League of Nations and in spite of the promise shown by its successor, the United Nations Organization, world unity has not been brought about. Inter-State relationships are not yet fully devoted to the attainment of global unification; they are still concerned with sectional and regional interests which may represent a necessary and experimental stage before the greater ideal is achieved, but each of which, in its turn, reveals the influence of geographical conditions.

Up to the end of the nineteenth century, inter-State affairs were largely dominated by "Imperial" considerations. Energetic, expansionist peoples sought outlets for their trade and territorial ambitions in the acquisition of lands beyond the limits of their own countries. In the result, vast Empires were built up, usually by haphazard methods and often because the representatives of one State happened to be first in the field of Empire building. Towards the end of that century, at least nominal claim had been established to almost the entire land surface of the globe by the various Powers. Any further territorial expansion could be made only at the expense of another organized State and would inevitably lead to resistance. Territorial imperialism was therefore replaced by economic imperialism whereby powerful States, prevented from acquiring new lands by the threat of war, sought to gain economic advantages by peaceful penetration and by the manipulation of a whole range of commercial and currency arrangements.

Rapidly increasing industrialism, with its concomitant in the growth of world trade, led to the evolution of what became known as "spheres of interest", which were vaguely if arbitrarily defined by the interested Powers largely according to the amount of pressure they were able to exert. Britain, France, Holland, Belgium, Germany, Italy and, more recently, the U.S.A., discovered that they possessed "vital interests" in various parts of the world. Treaties, often incorporating "most favoured nations" clauses, trade agreements, and a widespread network of consular representatives, were the means by which inter-State economic relationships were defined and implemented.

In practice, the system depended on extensive negotiations which necessitated a great deal of bargaining and understanding, but it could not have been operated in conditions other than those which existed throughout the last hundred years. First, the complicated commercial relationships of this period depended on the rapid growth of transportation facilities without which the volume of world trade would have remained at or near its earlier level. The growth of railways, the introduction of steamships and the invention of cargo-handling machinery were necessary prerequisites to the expansion of international trade. Second, the nineteenth century mercantile system was dependent on the existence of States at different levels of economic, social and political development. From the point of view of inter-State trade and its associated relationships and quite apart from purely internal exchanges of commodities, nineteenth century States fell into one of two categories. There were the "active" countries which led the way and organized world trade, and the "passive" countries which provided the bulk of the raw materials and were, in a sense, economic dependencies of their opposite numbers. Britain, France,

Holland and Belgium were the pioneers among the first group, but were later joined by Germany and the U.S.A. The European possessions in Africa, Asia, America and Australasia were in the main "passive", while China and South America fulfilled a similar function without being as closely tied politically.

This unequal partnership, directly based on the availability of seaways between the associated elements, was highly lucrative to the "active" States, more particularly after the Industrial Revolution had got into its stride, but its successful continuance relied on the "passive" regions remaining content to be "hewers of wood and drawers of water", and to accept their economically inferior position. Here it is necessary to draw a further distinction. In the Old World, India, China and South-East Asia were not only suppliers of commodities for West European consumption but were, in general, densely populated areas not only providing markets for European manufactured commodities, but also "safe" investments for the surplus capital which the "active" countries were accumulating. Hence there was little effort, apart from the Dutch East Indies, to colonize these territories. In the New World in the widest sense, i.e. including Australasia and Africa, the "passive" regions were thinly peopled at the beginning of the nineteenth century. They could become contributors to world trade only when their "empty lands" had been taken up by newcomers, the great majority of whom originated in Western and Central Europe.

This difference in geographical background, as between countries with dense populations and age-old economies and traditions, and countries with both low density and low total populations, but soon peopled by immigrants imbued with European ideas, gave rise to basic differences in political and economic outlook and therefore paved the way for different relationships with the "active" States.

The U.S.A. was the first to break away from European hegemony. This lead was followed by the South American republics, and the acquisition of dominion status by Canada, Australia, New Zealand and the Union of South Africa is in effect a compromise between complete independence and their continued existence as colonies. In short, the originally "passive" countries of the New World have achieved Statehood and that in an "active" form. In several cases and to a marked extent, they have closed their doors to further European immigration and all have ceased to be inferior, politically or economically.

In the Old World, the process of growing to Statehood among the "passive" countries was inevitably slower. The available agricultural areas have for long been fully occupied and internal economies were inimical to rapid changes. These lands were not possessed of vast "open spaces" wherein the iniative of European newcomers could apply new methods of large scale agricultural and mineral production. Their political, economic and cultural structures, such as they were, provided passive resistance to the infiltration of West European ideas and ways of life. The great majority of Indians, Chinese and Indonesians, in the aggregate amounting to half the world's population, were and remain a greater barrier to the extension of European influences than ever the great areas of the New World could have been.

Thus, even allowing for the progress of plantation agriculture in Africa and the East Indies, the New World countries have shown a dynamic quality in their evolution during the past century and a half, whereas the densely populated regions of Monsoon Asia, excluding Japan, have been characteristically static. Only in very recent times has anything approaching a real and widespread effort been made to throw off subjugation to West European political and economic hegemony. For the first time in history, in April 1947, an "Asian Relations Conference" was held in Delhi, and according to a correspondent of The Times[1] it " . . . may be regarded as an outcome of the decline of European political influence in the east, more particularly in South-East Asia, and the concomitant growth of national consciousness among Asian peoples".

It would appear, therefore, that the earlier pattern of relationships between "active", progressive, States and "passive", less rapidly evolving communities is giving way to a new set of inter-State relations. The nineteenth century concept of Imperialism, together with the economic exploitation of less

[1] The Times, April 15th, 1947.

highly organized lands, do not fit into the present scheme of things. If the twentieth century is to be "the Age of the Common Man", as publicists frequently assert, then the underfed, politically unorganized millions of Asia and Africa are equally entitled with their emancipated counterparts in Europe, America and Australasia to the benefits of such an age.

This revolution in inter-State relations is perhaps most cogently illustrated in the fact that India, Brazil, Egypt and Argentina are now "creditor" countries, whereas until the end of the last century, and in some cases even more recently, they were largely dependent on the availability of West European capital, mainly British, for their internal development. In effect, the first half of the twentieth century is marked by the steady spread of similarity in the political organization of States to an extent unknown previously. In the past, maturity in one or more States has always been coincident with immaturity and lack of organization in the rest of the world, so that the paths of territorial expansion were followed with relative ease. The State possessed of the power associated with political, military and economic organization, when it was based on adequate human and material resources, the latter including territory, was able to impose its will on States which were less well organized.

During and after the Age of Discovery the evolution of several dominant States or World Powers led to rivalry until their relationships were guided by the system which became known as the Balance of Power. Today, differential distribution of power remains. There are still World Powers and lesser powers, but the balance is far more delicate because the latter are asserting their claims to participation in world affairs to an extent undreamed of even fifty years ago. Frequently newspapers report that fifty or more nations are represented at an international conference, and the resentment which was expressed when the Great Powers were granted the right to veto decisions of the Assembly of the United Nations Organization is significant of the growing desire of the lesser powers to fulfil what they consider to be their functions in international relations.

For the political geographer, the meaning and value of this twentieth century phenomenon in world affairs rests on the possibility of a new alignment of States. In the past, groupings of territorial units have been imposed by more powerful States and have taken the form of empires or alliances for military purposes, either offensive or defensive. With the single exception of the British Empire, and that only in recent years, there has been no free association of States. Even the British Empire, as it was organized before the passing of the Statute of Westminster, was the result of conquest combined with the rewards of discovery and exploration. So also was the case with the Empires of France, Belgium, Holland and Germany. The U.S.A. found it necessary to fight their Civil War in order to impose unity, and at least economic and political pressure has been used to consolidate the Soviet Union.

Today the world is divided into States which may associate freely in their relations with each other on the political level, although their economic relations will continue to be guided by the necessity of feeding, clothing and housing their peoples, and therefore by the interchange of commodities of many kinds. In an ideal world, the relationships between these politically independent units would be integrated in a global pattern designed to facilitate the growth of a World Commonwealth, but such a unification, desirable as it may be, should not be expected in too short a time. There are still too many obstacles in the way of complete unity. Differences in political ideologies, in traditional outlook and culture, not to mention diversity in language and religion, all of which have developed over long periods of time, cannot be swept away overnight. Rather would it be wiser to proceed by way of an intermediary stage which may be shortly described as functional co-operation on a regional basis.

Mackinder's "geographical realities" suggest the framework within which such a grouping of States may come about and act as a prelude to the later growth of world unity, always provided that each of the regional groupings realizes that its interests will be best served by inter-group co-operation. The U.S.S.R. is already united, and what is more, has built up a regional grouping which includes what Professor Fawcett[1] has called the Western Transition Region. Western Europe, i.e. Europe west of a line from Stettin to Trieste, including the Iberian and Italian peninsulas, together perhaps with the Atlas Lands of North Africa, have much in common. The Middle East, largely coincident with the Arab World, including Syria, Lebanon, Iraq, Jordan, Egypt and possibly a re-organised Pakistan, suggests a second grouping among the marginal States, with increasing ties and more economic power than ever before because of its reserves of petroleum. In the Far East, broad similarities of climatic conditions associated with agricultural production and dense agrarian populations indicate close inter-relationships which may well be facilitated by the acquisition of more or less complete independence by India, Burma and Indonesia. Each of these last three groups possesses a high degree of contiguity with the added convenience of seaways, because of their shapes and disposition. The British Commonwealth and Empire might form a fifth association as it is already politically united, leaving the Americas as the sixth and last, but by no means the least, important group.

Each of the suggested unit-groups possesses vast material and human resources, and each contains within itself sufficient community of interest to make possible a satisfactory basis for functional co-operation, but clearly each would suffer from any attempts to achieve self-sufficiency in economic matters, since it would be in the interests of each group to promote the well-being of the remaining associations. In other words, a watertight grouping would be undesirable, and for two outstanding reasons. First, world trade, on which, in the last analysis, the well-being of mankind depends, cannot be satisfactorily carried on if economic barriers exist either between States or between groupings of them. Second, there are ties between States in different groups which will counterbalance any tendency to a restrictive regional economic development. It will be too much to expect the constituent States to sacrifice their sovereignty, more particularly in those cases where sovereign powers have only recently been acquired. The

[1] C. B. Fawcett, *op. cit.*, Fig. 4, p. 4.

suggestion here is that each association should develop as a political and economic federation which would provide a setting for both intraregional State relationships and for world relationships as between the groups.

It would be unwise to minimize the difficulties to be overcome and the dangers to be avoided, the greatest of the latter being the risk of one State establishing hegemony over the others in its group. But these problems are already present in the existing pattern in which many small States cannot hope to resist successfully the attempted domination of one Great Power without the assistance of another. On the other hand, world power would be more evenly distributed among these suggested groups, and once common action became possible within each region the danger of aggression in military or in economic affairs would probably be lessened. Clearly the establishment and implementation of such a scheme of federal regions is beyond the scope of Political Geography—that must remain the task of the statesmen. All that the political geographer can do is to indicate the geographical background against which any scheme of inter-State relationships must be placed. More and more knowledge of that background is being obtained, it might almost be said daily, and the outcome of this rapidly expanding awareness of the pattern of the earth's surface is a realization that the global physical environment has the quality of orderliness which the present arrangement of States appears to lack.

V

FRONTIERS AND BOUNDARIES

THE study of frontiers and boundaries is acknowledged to be an important branch of Political Geography, hence it is desirable to make clear, at the outset, the geographical connotations of the two terms. In common usage, they are synonyms; "international frontier" often means "international boundary" in the writings of politicians, historians and the like. An explanation of this interchangeability of terminology may be found in the fact that, until comparatively recent times, the limits of States and, with one or two exceptions, of the great Empires of the past, were ill-defined because of the lack of detailed knowledge of terrain and the absence of its exact cartographical representation. But with the advance in methods of surveying and mapping and with the evolution of the State to its present form, the great majority of boundaries are now not only clearly defined but are exactly demarcated on the ground.

Again, before the whole world had been parcelled out among the many States, large areas of its surface, then unfit for human occupation because of physical conditions, such as marshiness or forest cover, were frequently left as protective barriers behind which a young organization could develop in comparative safety. Gradually these barriers have been overcome in one way or another, and they have been incorporated in the territory of States; even in the great deserts, State control has been expanding until it meets the authority of other States, when dividing lines become necessary. Thus frontiers are zones or belts of territory, as is suggested by the terms, "Frontiers of Settlement", "Pioneer Fringes", etc. They possess area, great or small, and are subject to continued change as human agencies bring about modifications in their character and utilization. The time of large-scale territorial expansion into such frontier regions has gone; what remains is a period of intensification of settlement and land utilization, and of closer integration of the frontier area within the orbit of the State. This does not mean that the frontiers of the world have disappeared. On the contrary, they remain as marginal zones, and in some cases they still constitute regions of dispute between adjacent countries, and as such are disruptive elements in inter-State relations which the political geographer cannot afford to ignore.

While recognizing the continued existence of frontiers, in the sense in which the term is used above, it is also necessary to recognize that the character of the modern State necessitates the establishment of clear-cut limits to its area of authority and organization. For all its multifarious activities, of adminis-tration, of taxation, of defence, of trade, etc., etc., its territory must be clearly bounded, not by frontier areas, but by unmis-takable lines. Such lines are inter-State boundaries. Without them, the present system of States might well be reduced to a chaotic condition, since it would be impossible to know where the sovereignty of one State ended and that of another began. No longer is there much room for "neutral zones" or "no-man's-lands". With the exception of island States such as Australia, New Zealand and Iceland, all countries have land contacts with one or more other States, and some indication of the scale of these contacts and of the fragmentation of the earth's surface is given by Boggs' calculations[1], which show that the total length of inter-State boundaries (excluding coastlands) is 102,534 miles (165,013 kilometres).

No similar estimate of the world's frontiers can be made, for the simple reason that there is no agreement on their extent. They are transitional between geographical regions rather than between States, although international boundaries are often drawn within them. It is desirable and useful, therefore, to restrict the use of these two terms in order to avoid confusion of thought and of interpretation. Frontiers are areal, boundaries are linear, in character. The former may be correctly described as "natural", in so far as they are parts of the earth's surface; in some cases they fall into the category of geographical

[1] S. W. Boggs, *International Boundaries—A Study of Boundary Functions and Problems*, New York, 1940, Appendix A, pp. 207–218.

regions, inasmuch as they possess the quality of individuality based on their functions as transitional zones. The latter are artificial, since they are selected, defined and demarcated[1] by man, here in conformity with physical features of the terrain, there in complete disregard of such geographical factors.

Because of this difference, it is quite legitimate, for example, to describe the floor of the Rhine Rift Valley as a "natural frontier" between Germany and France, but the selection and use of the River Rhine as a part of the Franco-German boundary gives that line an artificial character; although the river is a "natural", i.e. physical feature, its use as a political boundary is artificial. Similarly there is some justification for describing the Alps as a natural frontier between Italy and France, but the boundary between the two countries represents the result of some centuries of adjustment between Italians and Frenchmen. Perhaps this difference is most emphatically illustrated by the fact that a frontier, be its character physical, linguistic, religious or ethnic, cannot be moved; it may change its character, it may lose much of its frontier function, but it must remain *in situ*. By contrast, boundaries are by no means immovable, as is indicated by the studies of Miss S. Saucerman,[2] who calculates that boundary changes arising out of the First World War in Europe alone led to the transfer of many thousands of square miles of territory.

This differentiation in the meanings of "frontier" and "boundary" helps to clarify many of the difficulties associated with the relationships which arise out of the juxtaposition of States. Frontiers have always existed, and geographers are only too familiar with the problems of their existence when they attempt to define regions. They have always possessed spatial extension, they have always occupied parts of the surface of the globe, but because of their transitional character they have defied exact definition.

The seas, the great forests, mountainous areas, extensive

---

[1] *Vide* S. B. Jones, *Boundary Making*, Washington, 1945, for a detailed examination of the technical terms used in connection with boundaries.

[2] S. Saucerman, *International Transfers of Territory in Europe*, Washington, 1937.

marshes, deserts both hot and cold, have served as barriers to human expansion and intercourse, but as a result of man's initiative and enterprise their separating functions have been greatly modified, and in no greater degree than by those efforts to organize human activities and utilization of resources which are manifested in the modern State. Thus the Appalachians were the western frontier of the original Thirteen Colonies in North America. Once valleyways through this barrier were discovered and effectively used, its frontier function was assumed by the prairies of the Middle West which, in their turn, were replaced by the mountain systems of the Far West, until eventually the "western spread of empire" reached the Pacific. Such continent-wide extension of the sway of States, equally well illustrated in the gradual eastward movement of Russian control in Asia, is no longer possible. Where frontiers have not been incorporated in States, the twentieth century problem is one of territorial adjustment, and is most clearly illustrated in efforts to set up boundaries within the disputed areas.

Three examples will serve to illustrate the point. In the Middle Zone of Europe, which lies between the Baltic and Adriatic Seas and has been appropriately called "The Eastern Marchlands of Europe",[1] exists a territory now containing approximately one hundred million people of very mixed ethnic and cultural character. For centuries this has been a borderland between East and West, open to the cultural and economic influences of both, subject to military conquest and persistently invaded both by armies and merchants because of its geographical location. Its terrain has provided no unsurpassable barriers, although it has tended to guide and direct human movements along certain lines. This region then has not been a barrier frontier, as its history amply demonstrates; rather has it exercised a bridging function and efforts to convert it into a *cordon sanitaire* have been notably unsuccessful. The twentieth century method of adjustment to frontier conditions here has been to establish a series of independent, but weak States, which have been little more than modern equivalents of the Carolingian "marks" of the ninth century. Politically

[1] *Vide* H. G. Wanklyn, *The Eastern Marchlands of Europe*, London, 1941.

Fig. 1

A Decade of Effort—Attempts to settle the Julian Boundary, 1914–24

76

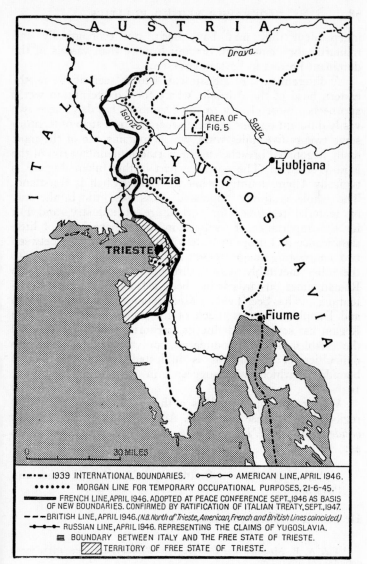

FIG. 2
Suggested Boundaries in the Julian March 1946–47

independent they may have been, but economically and militarily they have been not much more than vassals of the dominant Powers to East and West.

A different type of adjustment is to be seen at the north-eastern head of the Adriatic, where the Mediterranean world approaches most closely to the Danubian Lands. These two vastly different regions are here separated by a strip of territory some twenty-five miles wide, which contains one of the most easily negotiated breaches in the northern mountain rim of the Mid–World Sea. The northern part of this Julian Region[1] is typically Alpine country, while its southern half is Karstland. The whole is thinly populated, possesses little in the way of material resources for agriculture or industry, and but for the importance of its location would have been of little significance in European history. Just because it lies between two contrasting major regions, any expansion from one to the other inevitably passed through its gates, so that from Roman times onwards it has been a frontier, a zone of contention, and has been held by Mediterranean, Central European and Danubian Powers. Each of the possessors of the Julian Region has sought to define its territorial hegemony there by the establishment of boundaries, and some criterion of the difficulties of adjustment is indicated by the number of boundaries which were suggested in 1919–20 and again in 1946–47.[2]

Western Europe provides a third example of a frontier region in the case of what Ancel[3] called, "*Les Confins occidentaux*" of "*L'Europe Germanique*," and which he defines as:

" . . . toute la zone-frontière qui s'étend de la Suisse aux Pays-Bas".

He describes this territory as:

---

[1] *Vide* A. E. Moodie, *The Italo–Yugoslav Boundary*, London, 1945, for a definition of this region.

[2] Figures 1 and 2.

[3] J. Ancel, *Manuel Géographique de Politique Européenne*, Paris, 1940. Tome II, *L'Europe Germanique et ses bornes*.

"Enchevêtrement des paysages, opposition des genres de vie, traditions différentes dans le labeur: voilà, à première vue, les raisons d'être des contrastes, que la géographie accuse, mais que l'histoire amenuise."[1]

Human adjustment to these borderland features has resulted in the establishment of independent political entities at the northern and southern ends of this frontier region, but in its south-central section France and Germany come into direct contact, and their rivalry has caused repeated changes in the location of their common boundary.

Here satisfactory adjustment has obviously not been achieved, as is well shown in the history of Alsace. The evidence of place-names and the language of the majority of Alsatians reveal close ties with Germany, which are reinforced by economic links with that country by the great highways of the Rhine and its valley but, as Ancel pointed out,[2] its "spiritual affinities" are with French civilization. Linguistically, economically and culturally, it is therefore a marginal zone, subject to influences from East and West, and of necessity its people are torn by conflicting loyalties.

Conditions of human existence are not easy in these and similar marchlands. The ever-present possibility of boundary changes with their associated upheavals in political allegiance are inimical to both security and peaceful development, and seldom have the wishes of the inhabitants been consulted when decisions were made in the allocation of their territory. Indeed, the general rule has been that boundaries have been imposed in these frontier lands according to the success or failure of neighbouring States in their expansionist activities, and because such "settlements" are rarely mutually acceptable they tend to exacerbate conditions which are already difficult. Particularly is this so when intensive propaganda campaigns are conducted with a view to convincing the frontier peoples that their best interests lie in association with the State, which has temporarily succeeded in incorporating their land, because they stimulate "revisionist" claims by the State which, rightly or wrongly, considers the disputed territory as *terra irredenta*.

[1] *Op. cit.*, p. 9.
[2] *Op. cit.*, p. 51.

No aspect of international affairs reveals more clearly the limitations of mankind than the efforts to settle the disposal of these frontiers. Up to the present time decisions have often been reached by the exercise of force, and they have succeeded in sowing the seeds of further antagonisms which are only worsened by the fantastic claims sometimes put forward by the opposed parties. "Historic rights", "natural frontiers", "*terra irredenta*", are shibboleths which have all too often been used as excuses for aggrandisement. Political Geography can make a valuable contribution to human knowledge in this connection by careful study, on geographical lines, of these frontiers. The analysis of individual cases, such as those made by Goblet[1] and Ancel,[2] provide the bases for an evaluation of all the elements in the composition of these disputed territories.

Admittedly there is a vast amount of work to be done— the field is very wide—but that objective, detailed diagnosis is essential is indicated by the dismal failure in deciding the fate of frontiers without reference to their geographical character. That is why Goblet calls Political Geography a "science of peace". In the heat engendered by war, or even at the tables of international conferences, detachment and objectivity are difficult to obtain. Field investigation, supported by library studies, in times of peace, are the essential pre-requisites to the garnering of factual evidence. No two marchlands are identical. Their only resemblance is that they have been or may become zones of contention, of strain and of strife between the interested States. They do not fall into neat categories; each must be studied individually. Clearly the investigator must be free from nationalist bias; he should have full access to all the relevant documents, including maps, and his results should be available to the public. Probably the ideal procedure would be to organize these researches under the ægis of the United Nations Organization so that, in time, the relevant facts concerning all the world's major frontiers would be freely available for consultation.

[1] Y. Goblet, *Le Crépuscule des Traités*, Paris, 1934, translated as *The Twilight of Treaties*, London, 1936.
[2] J. Ancel, *op. cit.*

Much of what has been said above applies with equal force to boundaries, inasmuch as they frequently lie within frontiers, but there remains a fundamental difference which is inherent in their different characters and functions. Because it is a line, without significant area, an inter-State boundary cannot include material resources; it cannot be populated, nor can it be transitional. It represents an abrupt break between adjacent countries. It is specifically designed to separate and, as such, has no analogue in nature where strictly linear boundaries are noticeably absent. Its purpose is not that of the geographical frontier, which is to allow the mergence of one set of physical conditions with another, i.e. the passage of one physical environment to another, but to mark in no unmistakable manner the limit of the territory in which the State exercises its sovereign power with all the trappings which that exercise carries with it. In other words, a boundary defines the area within which the State's internal organization is developed, and along it different State systems of organization come into contact. It is therefore a political rather than a geographical feature, and its separating function depends largely on the degree of difference or of similarity between the organizations between which it lies.

"The location of the boundary therefore determines for millions of people the language and the ideas which children shall be taught at school, the books and newspapers which people will be able to buy and read, the kind of money they shall use, the markets in which they must buy and sell, and perhaps even the kinds of food they may be permitted to eat; it determines the national culture with which they shall be identified, the army in which they may be compelled to serve a term, the soil which they may be called upon to defend with their lives whether or not they would choose to defend it."[1]

There is nothing intrinsically evil or harmful in boundaries. As long as the world's population insists on grouping itself into a number of States, each demanding political independence but of unequal area, resources and power, and possessing

[1] S. W. Boggs, *op. cit.*, p. 5.

different economies and methods of organization, boundaries
will continue to be necessary as dividing lines between areas
of jurisdiction. How otherwise can the members of a State,
particularly those who live in the peripheral districts near
the margins, recognize the legal code under which they are
to live, pay their taxes to the right agency, and demand pro-
tection from the appropriate authority? That is why internal
boundaries are also necessary even in such a highly organized
and smooth-working State as the United Kingdom, where the
Local Government Boundary Commission has encountered
many grave difficulties in recommending some essential
changes. Why, then, it may be asked, do boundary disputes
occur so frequently and in so many parts of the world? The
answer to this question is related to two sets of geographical
conditions.

Firstly, the clearly demarcated inter-State boundary is a
recent addition to the "cultural landscape" and epitomizes
the growth of centralization of authority and power in the
State, as the normal machinery for the organization of human
activities; the more closely these internal activities are integrated, the greater the necessity for limits to be established
and made clearly recognizable. The need for such lines was
not felt until States had become sufficiently organized to
warrant definition of their areas of jurisdiction. In general, this
stage was not reached until the nineteenth century, although
historical atlases give the misleading impression that previously
parts of the earth's surface were divided by political boundaries
as precisely as they are today. There must have been check-
points where goods could be examined for tariff purposes,
but the very paucity of trade was one of the main reasons why
boundaries were not erected as they are now. As States assumed
their present form, and as world trade increased, it became
more and more necessary to adjust their relationships, and this
implied exact definition of their territories.

This process is not yet complete, and boundary disputes
fall into perspective when they are regarded as "the growing
pains" of an evolving world system which is still far from
reaching maturity. It would be unreasonable, therefore, to
expect such disputes to disappear immediately, but by

recognizing them as the results of efforts to adjust both the internal and external activities of contiguous States there is a better chance of finding solutions to boundary problems which have hitherto proved intractable.

In the second place, political boundaries are not merely territorial limits. It has been stressed in an earlier chapter that every State is an amalgam of land and people, so that its boundaries also enclose its population and their internal activities, and these two elements in its structure vary within a very wide range, even in adjacent countries. Where systems and levels of organization differ greatly on opposite sides of a boundary, there pressure is exerted on the dividing line and it becomes the locus of antagonism. Conversely, the existence of similar systems side by side reduces strain at the periphery of each.

These two extreme cases indicate that the presence or absence of disputes is the result of the function of the boundary, and that function derives not so much from the character and location of the line itself, but from the nature of the communities which it separates. If the latter are incompatible, conflict may arise; if they possess sufficient common interests, and exhibit good will towards each other, then dispute is avoidable. The role of political boundaries in international affairs depends, therefore, on the degree of adjustment achieved by the various States to the distributional pattern in which they exist, as well as on the level of organizational development within each of them.

Regarded from this point of view, every boundary problem represents an attempt on the part of one or more States to find a *modus operandi* in the lengthy process of arriving at such a closely interwoven community of interests that dividing lines will become obsolete and unnecessary. Such a Utopian state in both external and internal relationships is not yet in sight, so that boundary disputes must be expected wherever incompatibility occurs between adjacent countries, but some cause for optimism may be found in those instances where unilateral imposition of inter-State limits is being replaced by bilateral and even multilateral agreement. This is a step in the right direction towards the elimination of ill-feeling and bitterness among States in regard to their common limits, because it suggests that emphasis is being laid on the nature, needs and potentialities of the State rather than on the precise character and location of its boundaries.

In other words, the mental attitude of politicians towards the State and its boundaries is becoming more comparable with that of the geographer towards regions. The latter thinks in terms of the individuality, area, shape and content of a region first, and then seeks to define its limits. Throughout the nineteenth century, statesmen sought to establish territorial boundaries first, and then concentrated on developing the State inside those confines, with the result that friction grew, particularly in marginal areas, if only because once the dividing lines were set up they tended to be regarded as rigid fixtures which could only be altered as the outcome of war. This failure to recognize the mutability of boundaries, or possibly the fears which such a recognition engenders, gave rise to attempts to reinforce their function of separation. Tariff walls were erected and fortifications were set up in a vain effort to achieve the mutual exclusiveness of political entities, whereas rapidly increasing population, extending inter-State trade and the growth of means of communication which made that trade possible required the removal of obstacles. It is significant that until the end of the nineteenth century passports were unknown and people could move freely from one country to another without all the irksome formalities which are now necessary.

Thus, international boundaries have become the outward and all too visible evidence of the maladjustment of political and economic relationships between States. It follows that the greater the number of States on a given part of the earth's surface, the greater the combined lengths of the boundaries must be, and, therefore, the greater the possibility of inter-State friction, and so, in turn, the hope of creating both political and economic integration is proportionately reduced. As the numbers of independent political entities are unevenly distributed throughout the world, the parts which are most partitioned are the most likely areas to produce boundary disputes.

Political geographers are indebted to Mr. S. W. Boggs for

reducing this generalization to more precise terms by his calculations of the total lengths of international boundaries, not only for the world as a whole but also for the individual continents. Conscious of the relative unimportance of mere length, he has related his linear measurements to area and population. By multiplying the number of miles of boundary per thousand square miles by the population per square mile, he arrives at a tentative index of "the interruptive factor— the nuisance effect—of boundaries",[1] and expresses in a numerical form the variations in degree of the division of the continents, which the political map of the world shows with much less clarity, because the continents themselves vary greatly in area. Aware also of the invalidity of the traditional convention of the line of the Ural Mountains as a boundary between Asia and Europe, he makes allowance for the Euro–Asiatic character of the U.S.S.R., so that his index numbers fall into the following order:[2]

Europe (excluding U.S.S.R. and Iceland)	1400
Asia (excluding the Philippines)	190
South America	33
Africa (excluding Madagascar and the boundaries of the Union of South Africa with other British territories)	30
North America (including Central America and the West Indies, but excluding Greenland and the Canada–Labrador boundary)	23

Two points of interest to the political geographer stand out from this classification. First, the extreme contrast between the Heartland and the "marginal" lands referred to in Chapter IV above, makes possible the economic and political development of the Soviet Union without obstruction by international boundaries. The Heartland, in so far as it is represented by Russian territory, occupies the largest extent of continuous land surface in the world, and there is no other comparable area under one unified political system. That is one reason why that Union has been able to apply large-scale methods of

[1] S. W. Boggs, *op. cit.*, p. 16.
[2] *Ibid.*, Table I, p. 13.

economic development more rapidly than was possible elsewhere. It also supplies a partial explanation of the vast potential of Russian influence in the world.

Second, continental Europe west of the Soviet boundary is more minutely partitioned than any other continent, great or small. Even in total mileage of boundaries, it exceeds the whole of North America, including the West Indies,[1] but when length is considered with area and population, Europe is unique among the continents in the extent to which its surface is divided among independent States.

The reasons for this unusual fragmentation are many and complex, and they are related to historical rather than to geographical factors, but certain of the latter have played their part. The peninsular character of the continent has laid it open, on its eastern side, i.e. on its landward flank, to the infiltrations of peoples from the Asiatic land-mass. The exact reasons for the migrations of peoples from the East are still debatable, but there is no dispute as to the relative ease with which they were able to move westwards into Europe. Then the European Plain and the Danubian Lands provided corridors along which they could pass.

Again, differences in geological structure and in resultant terrain give a great variety of physical environments in Europe, while climatic conditions, without precluding human activities because of too much heat or excessive cold, are sufficiently diverse to encourage a wide range of plants, and consequently of agricultural production. The deep penetration of arms of the sea, more pronounced here than in any other continent, and justifying its description as "a peninsula of peninsulas", combined with the diversity of land forms and climatic effects to provide primitive Europe with a mosaic of habitats, the like of which is unknown elsewhere, and the lack of physical uniformity paved the way for the variety of States which gradually evolved. Within the different habitats, communities gradually established themselves and made the land their own by sustained efforts in cultivating the soils, clearing the forests and draining the marshes. On the whole, their exertions were

[1] Europe west of U.S.S.R. 14,846 miles. Africa 28,113 miles. Asia 26,11? miles, South America 18,961 miles, and North America 11,433 miles.

satisfactorily rewarded and they became attached to their lands to such an extent that the seeds of a kind of patriotism were sown.

Although this relationship was by no means confined to Europe, it was in this continent that close ties with the soil and a common way of life in each habitat gave rise to the phenomenon known as nationalism which, during the last two centuries, has been a decisive factor in the formation of European States which are not comparable in number with the original regional habitats because encroachment and amalgamation were characteristic of the time when frontiers between the early communities were being overcome. Nevertheless, the outlines of the pattern of occupancy, as indicated by the physical geography of early Europe, is still apparent in the plethora of States today, and not least among the contributions of this continent to human progress is the idea of the nationalist State with its corollary of international boundaries.

Everywhere in the inhabited world the European model is being copied, with modifications arising out of differences in the physical environment. In the New World the system was introduced and developed by immigrants from Europe. In Monsoon Asia nationalism has taken root in both conquered and independent countries, while in Africa, south of the Sahara, native peoples are beginning to anticipate the time when they will be able to enjoy the mixed blessings of national independence. This planetary spread of what is, in effect, a way of life may well lead to a further development of boundary disputes of which Europe already has a number commensurate with its degree of partition. Such a threat to world peace and well-being can be reduced by a recognition of the fact that controversial boundary problems are a symptom of internal or external maladjustments.

As the modern European States assumed their present forms and pattern, the need for dividing lines became apparent and, in the absence of detailed knowledge and of accurate cartographic records of the continent's surface, men seized on clearly recognizable physical features as boundaries. Coastlines, rivers, mountain crests, especially where they exerted a separating function, were relatively permanent and already in existence, so that it is not surprising that they were soon appropriated as "natural" boundaries. They were there for all to see, and while the State was loosely-knit, still far removed from the stage when all its resources were to be exploited in detail and all its people's activities organized on a high level, no doubt some of these boundaries were temporarily satisfactory.

Their selection for use as limits was, however, unfortunate for at least two reasons. In the first place, once boundaries are established, they are not easily changed, as the unsuccessful struggles for revision in the inter-war years prove; once a State has been successful in achieving what its people consider to be a satisfactory limit, however unsatisfactory that limit may appear to others, then major changes are resisted by all the means at the disposal of the successful community. Second, and of more importance to the political geographer, areas of human occupancy, whether they be States or not, are nowhere precisely defined by physical features, with the possible exception of coastlines.[1] Whatever the basis of differentiation between human societies, ethnic origin, religion, language, economic activities, political systems, or a combination of two or more of them, these cementing agencies do not suddenly stop short at a river, a mountain range, a lake or a marsh; still less do they cease to function at any line which may be laid down in relation to physical features, and it will be recalled that the essential quality of a boundary is its linear character.

Because of this overlapping and intermingling of human activities, the fixation of limits must be accompanied by a degree of arbitrariness, but is less likely to be mutually acceptable when tied to physical features not exerting a separating function. The traditional European method of using so-called physical boundaries has become obsolete; their unsatisfactory character is demonstrated by their reinforcement by tariff barriers and military works. In general, they neither separate States effectively nor do they provide unimpeded facilities for intercourse; in detail, they are the

---

[1] In any case, these are national, not international, boundaries.

cause of friction because all too frequently they disregard human activities and interests.

Looked at on small-scale relief maps, rivers and mountain ranges give the impression of usefulness as dividing lines, but more comprehensive knowledge shows that often the areas in which they occur possess a kind of unity which the physical map does not reveal. Mountainous regions do not always exert the barrier function which is all too often associated with them. Once the need for transmontane contact is felt by adjacent communities, ways and means of bringing it about are soon found or made, and not necessarily by complicated engineering feats such as the roads and railway tunnels which link Germany and Italy or France and Spain, nor by air routes, such as that which connected India and China, "over the hump", during the Second World War. For example, the morphology of mountain terrain restricts agricultural activities by the inadequacy of land suitable for arable farming, so that its inhabitants utilize the mountain pastures as an element in their agrarian economy. Now such pastures are not limited to one side or the other of a crest. Frequently, where elevation is not prohibitive, they occur on the crest itself, and in the course of centuries, the valley dwellers have incorporated their use in the system known as transhumance. When an inter-State boundary is set up in such an area, the pastures may be separated from the permanently inhabited valley floors at considerable loss to the peasant farmers. The Polish–Czecho-slovak boundary in the Tatra,[1] and the Italo–Jugoslav boundary in the Julian Alps, both of which came into being after the First World War, provide numerous examples of this separation of elements in the rural economy of mountain regions.

Similarly mountainous areas do not necessarily prohibit the spread of language, religion or customs, as is abundantly illustrated in Europe and elsewhere. Switzerland is trilingual, German is the language of Austria, Roumanian is spoken on the Magyar side of the Transylvanian Alps, while the distribution of the Basques athwart the Western Pyrenees is an

[1] *Vide* Figs. 3 and 4.

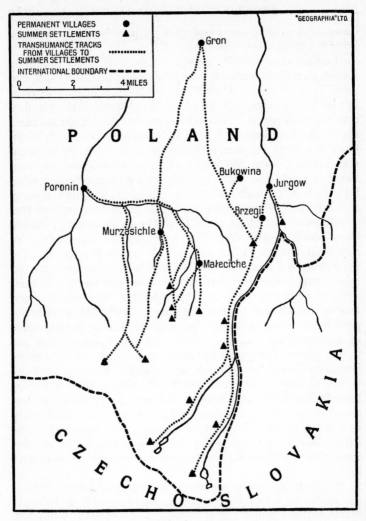

FIG. 3

Permanent Villages and Summer Settlements of a part of the Polish Tatra. The villagers of Jurgow were forced to share in the use of the Alpine meadows which were traditionally owned by the people of Bukowina and Brzegi and suffered accordingly

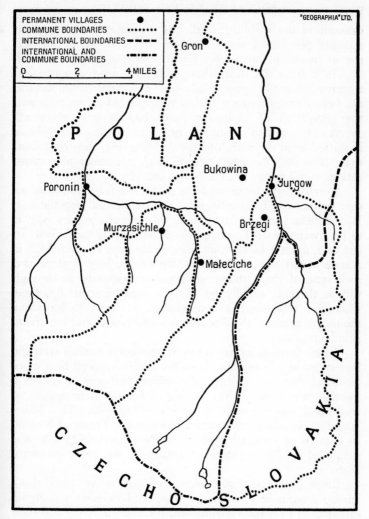

FIG. 4

Commune Boundaries in a part of the Polish Tatra. The Polish-Czechoslovak Boundary of 1919 was drawn so that the Commune of Jurgow was divided into two unequal parts and the villagers were deprived of their pastoral rights in the southern, mountainous, part of their commune

91

example of the inability of all but the highest mountains to separate peoples of similar ethnic origin. It seems that the use of mountain ranges for the establishment of boundaries is a relic from the time when such areas were geographical frontiers, scantily populated and relatively unimportant, i.e. before transhumance had developed, before tourism and the generation of hydro-electricity had become important sources of wealth of mountain peoples. As soon as emphasis is shifted from the march to the dividing line, then complications arise and the aggregate of local grievances may cause serious conflict between the States concerned.

Moreover, the location of the actual line is by no means an easy matter and frequently requires complicated negotiations. Is it to be an irregular line joining the highest summits, or is it to be a watershed? The two are seldom exactly coincident. In any case, a watershed is only a *line on the map*. In the field, it is a zone of varying width depending on the height, slope and rock type of the district concerned. Particularly in through valleys there is usually an area of indeterminate drainage, wherein a watershed is non-existent, or again, in limestone mountains much of the drainage is subterranean and the divide is indeterminable.

Where boundaries are set up in mountain country strategic factors are also important. If such a line is imposed by a more powerful State on another, the former will seek to obtain a location which will secure military advantage irrespective of traditional rights and distribution of peoples. The Italo–Jugoslav boundary,[1] as it was defined in the Treaty of Rapallo in 1921, is an excellent example of how the dividing line was delimited to the military advantage of the more powerful State.

River boundaries are even less satisfactory than those among mountains. Drainage basins tend to exert a unifying rather than a separating influence, because the rivers and their valleys provide lines of movement which foster social and commercial intercourse. Basins such as those of the Lower Thames, the Seine and the Vienna Basin have indeed been

[1] *Vide* Fig. 5.

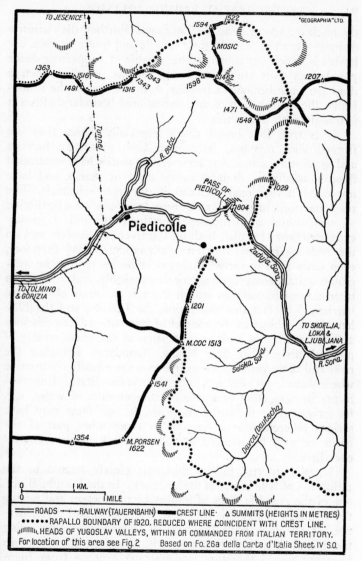

FIG. 5
The Piedicolle Section of the Rapallo Line

the nuclear areas of some modern States. Further, the vicinities of most rivers, at least in their middle and lower courses, are lowlands which are usually more capable of supporting dense populations than are mountainous regions, so that when a drainage basin becomes a frontier, as in the case of the Rhinelands, the delimitation of an international boundary within it is fraught with difficulties.

It is true that broad rivers, especially where they are fringed with marshes, have been both protective barriers and separating zones, but engineering works have controlled flood possibilities, drained many areas of marsh, and have improved navigational facilities in the river channels. The result has been, in general, an increase in population, a furthering of agricultural and industrial productivity, and a greatly expanded flow of traffic, both on the rivers themselves and on the roads and railways which use their valleys. Today, therefore, even more than in earlier times, river basins tend to be integrated units, demographically or economically, and to establish international boundaries within them is to create obstructive barriers. The fact that the Rhine, the Danube and the Elbe have been subject to the control of international commissions at various times is itself an indication of the undesirability of political division in their basins. Boundaries following the river and those running transverse to it are equally obstructive where there is no joint action by the riverine States. Improvements in navigation or increased consumption of water, e.g. for irrigation or industrial purposes, in one State may have serious repercussions in regions in some other part of the basin, or may be reduced in value by lack of river control elsewhere.

Egypt's interest in the Sudan is clearly related to the utilization of Nile Water in the latter area. In the Danube Basin, one of the possible ways of improving production and raising the standard of living is by the intensification and diversification of cropping with the help of irrigation systems using the Danube's water. Excessive withdrawal of this water in Hungary would therefore evoke strong protests from Jugoslavia and Roumania.

Again, river control in one State may easily cause increased flooding in downstream States by speeding up the rate of discharge of the river. It is not difficult, for instance, to imagine the friction which would be caused if an international boundary crossed the Mississippi in the latitude of Memphis, and the vast irrigation system of Sind might have been seriously interrupted but for the existence of a unified political control in almost the whole of the basin of the Indus.[1] Short of including each major basin in a State, and in the absence of genuine inter-State co-operation, the only solution to these difficulties lies in international control, but even that compromise cannot remove all the hindrances which river boundaries present.

There is another important geographical aspect of the use of rivers as boundaries, and for this purpose lakes, estuaries and minor arms of the sea may be considered as extensions of rivers. Where it is decided that a river shall be a boundary, the problem arises of defining the location of the dividing line, which clearly cannot be the whole water body. It must be defined with relation to some part or parts of the river.[2] Generally one of three lines is adopted, the median line, the middle of the navigable channel, or one of the shorelines. In the first case (the term is rarely used in boundary agreements), the line is related to the horizontal plane of the river, and may be defined as the line joining all points which are equidistant from the nearest points on opposite shores, and its location requires careful mathematical calculation. Its adoption leads to an equal division of the surface of the water, but not to an equal division of its volume.

In the second case, the navigable channel, i.e. usually the belt of continuously deepest water, follows a sinuous course, now approaching one bank, now swinging towards the other, and therefore crossing and re-crossing the median line. Moreover the navigable channel may change its position in the river by the same process as the latter itself may change its course.

[1] The sharing of the Punjab between Hindustan and Pakistan may have disastrous effects in this part of India, which is dependent on the Indus system for its irrigation water, unless precautionary measures are included in the plan for the political division of India.

[2] On rivers as boundaries, see Boggs, *op. cit.*, Chapter X.

The adoption of either of these lines necessarily causes complications in the use of the river, in access to its banks and, where necessary, in the maintenance of flood prevention works and navigational facilities.

The shoreline is less frequently used than the navigable channel as a boundary. It also is liable to change, but it is generally more clearly marked than the two previous lines. One interesting case will suffice to show the difficulties inherent in such a selection. The Pact of Rome of 1924[1] defined the Italo–Jugoslav boundary in the vicinity of Fiume and laid it down that the line should follow the western bank of the Fiumara Channel of the River Eneo so that sovereign power over the lower, navigable channel was given to Jugoslavia, but, " . . . this sovereignty shall not extend to the left[2] bank, from the base to the extreme edge of the coping, as this bank forms the frontier limit of Italian territory." This meant that maintenance of the bank of what was to all intents and purposes a Jugoslav river was in Italian hands and the right shore could not legally be used for the construction of quays by either party. The intended effect was to force Jugoslavia to use Italian owned docking facilities in Fiume, but the actual result was to force the Jugoslavs to extend their docks and equipment at Split and Metković much further south on the Adriatic coast.

Difficulties also arise in the determination and use of median lines and navigable channels in lakes, more particularly in those cases where the water bodies are valuable arteries of commerce or contain useful fishing-grounds. The Great Lakes of North America provide the best examples, partly because, in the aggregate, they constitute the largest area of fresh water in the world, partly because they are a geographical frontier between Canada and U.S.A., but mainly because boundary disputes connected with them have been settled peacefully and to the mutual satisfaction of both parties.

It would be a mistake to think that water boundaries give

---

[1] League of Nations Treaty Series, Vol. XXIV, 1924.

[2] "Left" here clearly meant "right" and is an example of misuse of terms which is sometimes found in treaty arrangements.

rise to problems only when international dividing lines are concerned, although such cases receive greater publicity and attention. Nevertheless, internal boundaries, i.e. boundaries of the internal administrative divisions of States, are frequently tied to rivers, as a brief examination of the large-scale maps of any national survey will show. In Britain, county and parish limits are often defined in this way, and a change in the course of a river is sometimes indicated by the fact that a boundary occasionally diverges from the present channel to follow an earlier course. Similarly in other countries, rivers and lakes are used and the dangers in this usage, where appropriate precautions are not taken, are well illustrated by Lawrence Martin's study of the Wisconsin–Michigan boundary where it runs through Lake Michigan.[1] In this case, four years of litigation at the highest national level were necessary to rectify a previous legal decision.

These are but some of the problems inherent in the use of physical features as political boundaries. Nowhere do they provide complete and continuous dividing lines. The only apparent advantage in their employment is that they are recognizable in the landscape and are generally familiar to the borderland inhabitants, but this asset can be equally well obtained by modern methods of boundary marking. They came into use for boundary purposes when the State fulfilled a function different from that of today, and when knowledge was inadequate for boundary delimitation and demarcation. Unfortunately their adoption has become a tradition, particularly in Europe. The excessive fragmentation of this continent, the result of a long and complicated historical evolution, can no longer be considered as a justification of their use in this connection. If then physical features are inadequate and unsatisfactory as political boundaries, what alternatives are available? The answer to this question is twofold, but each part of it is closely related to the character of the political entities and their territorial bases which, under present circumstances, demand delimitation.

[1] L. Martin, "The Second Wisconsin–Michigan Boundary Case in the Supreme Court of the United States, 1932–1936." *Annals of the American Association of Geographers*, June 1938, Vol. xxviii, No. 2.

Geographers and students of political science alike seldom appear to realize that the world pattern of States, and in consequence their boundaries, have been imposed on a pre-existing physical background and that this imposition has carried the quality of arbitrariness. The search for "natural boundaries" has been nugatory because linear limits do not exist in nature, although in many cases the expressed desire for them has served as a cloak for expansionist activities, in particular where physical features appear to give strategic or economic advantages.

This is especially true of Europe with its congeries of States, of great variety in area and population, and where too much history is remembered in so far as claims to boundaries are often based on an earlier pattern of organization, which is out of tune with present conditions. In the "New World", including the Americas, Africa and Australia, the relative "emptiness" of the land, the absence of nationalism and the almost complete lack of geographical knowledge resulted in the establishment of geometrical boundaries which were satisfactory enough in the colonial stage, since there was abundant space for expansion, and pressure on these wholly arbitrary dividing lines was non-existent. On the whole, these boundaries, whether international or internal, have continued to be satisfactory divides, but not because of any intrinsic merits they possess. Whether they have been parts of meridians, or of other great circles, or of lines of latitude, or whether they have been drawn parallel to coastlines, as in the case of the Alaska–British Columbia boundary, their successful functioning has been an expression of the character and relationships of the States which they divide, and these have, in general, been primarily concerned with their own internal organization and consolidation.

It remains to be seen if such boundaries will continue to be mutually acceptable as the various States become more highly developed, more closely populated and take a greater share in world affairs. The Canada–U.S.A. boundary is continuing to function smoothly, but in South America, where it is significant that most of the States' limits are associated with physical features, there have been numerous boundary disputes, some of which are not yet settled. As an alternative to rivers, mountain crests and the like, then, geometrical lines are satisfactory boundaries provided that the relationships between adjacent States are such as to avoid marked pressure on their peripheries. They cannot be considered as satisfactory alternatives in regions such as Europe, where the uneasy balance between countries is partly the result of their historical evolution and partly the result of their confinement in a relatively small area.

Here, more than in any other continent, is it necessary to take into consideration the content and character of the States when defining their boundaries, especially from the point of view of facilitating the smooth working of their inter-relationships. The problem of territorial delimitation would doubtless be eased by the successful creation of a United States of Europe, inasmuch as it would reduce the status of boundaries from the international to the internal level, but there seems to be little hope of this change even in the non-Slav parts of the continent. In the meantime some *modus operandi* is necessary. Geometrical lines and physical features do not provide appropriate boundaries here, because they do not conform to the requirements of the various States.

Most of Europe's boundaries are what Boggs has called "anthropogeographic" in character, because they represent attempts to enclose groups of people and their territory according to one or more aspects of homogeneity within each group. The striking fact about these lines is that, while they are the most accurately delimited and demarcated and the most jealously guarded of all boundaries, the unity of the entities which they define is at least open to question and always difficult to assess. Moreover, the degree of unity tends to weaken towards the State's periphery if only because of contacts with other States, yet it is in these transitional areas, often impossible to delimit exactly, that political, including administrative purposes, demand that precisely demarcated boundaries be established.

That is an outstanding paradox which confronts the student of Political Geography and it helps to explain the intractable character of many boundary disputes. It also explains why all international divides, except those imposed by superior military power, express an element of compromise between conflicting claims, and further, why the recommendations of commissions of experts set up to advise peace conferences and the like are seldom accepted and acted upon in full.

As an alternative to the "natural" boundary and to the geometric line, anthropogeographic boundaries are becoming increasingly important, not only in Europe but in other parts of the world, notably in the Middle East and in India. Their acceptance was implied in the establishment of the principle of self-determination which was first put forward as a universal doctrine at the Peace Conference which followed the First World War. This theory, however revolutionary it may be, and whatever difficulties it may cause in inter-State relationships, is the operative factor in the continuance of existing States and in the creation of new political units. Its importance for the political geographer rests on the recognition of the geographical bases, both physical and human, of the self-determined State and, by implication, the delimitation of these bases by political boundaries. These are by no means easy tasks.

The physical setting of the State rarely possesses geographical unity, but its human content is even more diverse, and the factors which differentiate the inhabitants of one country from those of others are often intangibles only directly observable in their outward manifestations, and because they lie in the realm of ideas more often than not, they cannot be confined to any one selected territorial area. Gauld[1] expresses the point neatly when he writes, "What binds a people into a nation-state is a compound of sentiment and tradition and geographical propinquity." "Sentiment" is manifested in language, religion, patriotism and political ideas; "tradition" is the resultant, conscious or otherwise, of historical factors and conditions, but rarely, if ever, are the people who share these sentiments and traditions found in close geographical propinquity in a naturally well-defined area.

[1] W. A. Gauld, *Man, Nature and Time*, London, 1946, p. 204.

Large-scale transfers of territory and population may be one way of giving greater clarity to the present confused pattern of the distribution of "nationality", but the cost is heavy in view of the hardships suffered by the people concerned and, in any case, organized mass migrations, whether voluntary or compulsory, provide no guarantee that all the boundary problems will be solved for the very reason indicated above; i.e. no yardstick for the accurate measurement of the psychological factors in the structure of a State has yet been devised.

On the other hand, should criteria for the delimitation of the distribution of these psychological phenomena be discovered the general situation would not be greatly eased in so far as the areas occupied by peoples of different languages, religions, ways of life, etc., are not coincident, so that at least the problems of minorities would remain. As Azcárate[1] points out, "No tracing of frontiers could suppress the existence of national minorities and assure the national homogeneity of the peoples of each State."

Homogeneity, unattainable as it is, should not be regarded as the ideal for the organization of human societies. Just as heterogeneity in conditions of terrain and in the material resources is a contributory factor to the prosperity of a country, so human diversity, provided it is encouraged by tolerance and freedom, may be rightly regarded as a source of material and moral well-being. It follows from this that the use of religion, language, tradition and "race" as bases for the delimitation of States is now outmoded; in point of fact, they have never been much more than cloaks for territorial aggrandisement. But boundaries are still necessary in the world as it is, and they will continue to be drawn in frontier zones; as long as States are antagonistic in their relationships, boundary disputes will still arise.

Only when the inhabitants of all States appreciate and put into practice the view that their interests, cultural and economic, are best served by close interdependence will boundaries cease to exert separating functions. It will be freely admitted

[1] P. de Azcárate, *op. cit.*, p. 7.

that this prospect is remote, but its attainment is the only way of avoiding continued and costly disputes. When that happy day arrives, political geographers will not find it necessary to debate the respective merits of physical, geometric and anthropogeographic boundaries.

VI

COMMUNICATIONS

FEW, if any, fields of human endeavour have recorded greater progress than that which is concerned with the establishment and maintenance of means of communication. Facilities for the movement of people, goods and ideas are abundantly available to mankind in modern times and play a vital part in human activities at every level, local, regional, national and international. They are of great importance to the political geographer because they are the channels by which and through which organization, both of States and of international affairs, is developed; without them, the internal activities of States could not have reached their present stages of evolution, and international relations would be hampered. Civilization itself is largely the product of circulation.

The value of communications is indicated by the comprehensive range of services embraced by the term "circulation". They include not only the normal forms of transport, such as those by land, sea and air, but also telecommunications, pipelines, which are becoming increasingly used for the distribution of such commodities as water, oil and natural gas, and cable systems for the transmission of electricity.

In this widest sense, modern communications facilitate the movement of commodities, people and ideas, within and between States. They exercise a unifying influence which varies in direct proportion to the density and carrying capacity of the various systems. Few physical obstacles remain to be overcome, but, paradoxically enough, artificial barriers are still common, and provide the greatest hindrance to that free flow without which circulation cannot exert its maximum beneficial influence. That is why the study of communications is an important aspect of Political Geography. Their establishment and growth are intimately related to the internal and external policies of States. Political, strategic, economic and cultural factors are all involved, and the increasing complexity of relationships, national and international, demands the smooth working of communications of all kinds.

This idea of the basic importance of circulation in the development of human activities is no new thing. From the dawn of history, communities which possessed the power of mobility were advantageously placed with regard to other peoples. Egypt, the Mesopotamian Empires, and China utilized their rivers as highways for commercial as well as military purposes. The city-states of the Ægean were pioneers in the use of sea transport, and their example was followed by Rome. Unlike its predecessors, however, Rome set a new standard in empire-building and administration by combining organized land and sea transport on a large scale. By destroying Carthage, the Romans gained command of the Mediterranean and its route-ways, and integrated their conquests by establishing a system of roads such as had never been seen before and which remained unsurpassed until many centuries later.

In this respect the Romans made a unique contribution to human knowledge and experience, more particularly as regards territorial organization. The statement that "All roads lead to Rome" was literally true, because, first, there were no other roads comparable with those which bound the constituent parts of the Empire to the nuclear region in the Plain of Latium, and second, because "all roads" included both land and sea routes which were the only known means of communication at that time. The Pax Romana disappeared for many reasons, but outstanding among them was the replacement of the Roman system of imperial organization by many separate communities of immigrant "barbarians". Out of their settlements and conquests a multitude of petty societies grew by devious and painful processes.

This substitution of anarchy for order in the known world is perhaps the best illustration of the vital part which is played by organized communications in the lives of men. For centuries after the fall of Rome the use of organized mobility along well-defined routes largely disappeared. There was still some more or less sporadic movement on the bordering seas, especially where the frequency of islands and the articulation of coastlines were of assistance to navigators, but technical skill in ship construction and navigation made very slow progress.

Under such circumstances law and order could not be maintained except within the reach of the strong arm of a local magnate, so that society, where it was organized at all, fell into the bondage of the feudal system which was characterized by excessive territorial fragmentation and almost complete lack of contact even between adjacent communities. Such a Dark Age could be enlightened and finally replaced only by the re-institution of widely spread communications, but this involved both a revolution in the medium of transport and a re-orientation in the minds and outlook of men. Such is the yardstick for measuring the achievements of the pioneers like Henry the Navigator and da Gama, whose ocean voyages heralded the Age of Discovery and the initiation of a new phase in the development of communications, a phase which was to culminate in global circulation.

The discoveries of the fifteenth and sixteenth centuries, followed by the slow opening up of the new lands, set in train a series of developments which have not yet reached their full fruition. In addition to providing a vast new range of commercial possibilities and an enormous scope for emigration and home-seeking, they finally broke down what had previously been the greatest single physical barrier to circulation, the oceans. For the first time the bordering seas and the open oceans were effectively united in the sense that they could be used to connect the adjoining land masses, and the States which had begun to grow up on their shorelands were not slow to realize their political advantages. In the words of Vidal de la Blache:[1]

"Avec la fusion des domaines maritimes en un ensemble illimité de mers et d'océans de nouvelles perspectives politiques apparaissaient dès l'aurore des temps modernes. Les rêves d'hégémonie mondiale, dont la réalisation s'était toujours heurtée a l'exiguïté des continents et aux limites imposées par leur configurations géographiques, ne semblent plus une chimère."

[1] P. V. de la Blache, *Principes de Géographie Humaine*, Paris, 1922, p. 269.

The pioneers of the Age of Discovery laid the foundations of political systems which they could scarcely have foreseen. Quite apart from the commercial and naval developments which followed their voyages and discoveries, they paved the way for the establishment of great maritime empires, the leaders of which soon came to appreciate the value of sea power as the means of securing and expanding their territories. For the first time in history the oceans became the world's highways. Colonies were founded, trade increased rapidly, and the ships of the West European maritime Powers brought into contact territories which had previously been inaccessible to each other. Such a revolutionary development demanded a re-orientation in the minds of the men who were responsible for the formulation of the policies which were to guide the growth of the new world relationships. Their eyes were temporarily turned away from the lands to the oceans where the most enlightened of them realized that the future greatness of their countries lay.

But once the new lands were discovered, once the colonies were set up, it became clear that further territorial and economic expansion necessitated a parallel development of land communications if the maximum benefits were to be derived from the human activities on the oceans and their immediate shore-lands. Efforts in this direction were first centred on unsurfaced roads, barely more than tracks, and it was not until the inventions of the nineteenth century led to the application of first iron and then steel that the railway and the steamship became the integrating factors in a vast new global network of communications which made possible unrivalled progress in productiveness and material prosperity, and also created innumerable problems in the construction and organization of the new means of circulation.

The corollary of all this progress was a marked quickening of the tempo of international competition, both in the acquisition of territory and of markets, but also for supremacy in world trade through control of routes on sea and on land. With the single exception of China, and that for special reasons, all the major States of the twentieth century have attempted, with varying success, to create powerful merchant marines and appropriate naval fleets to protect them, and have designed their railway systems to tie up with their overseas communications. This headlong race between the major Powers, in some cases directly under the aegis of the Governments concerned, in others largely as the result of private enterprise, has, in general, conferred benefits on mankind in so far as it has stimulated the production and distribution of all kinds of commodities, but inasmuch as the motivating force has been unilateral, it has resulted in the establishment of numerous artificial barriers to circulation.

The twentieth century has surely demonstrated the suicidal character of this international strife and, in consequence, the overriding necessity of removing barriers to the free flow of goods and people. The uneven distributional pattern of productiveness in the world, the differences in level of economic and political organization in the various States, call for greater, not less, intercommunication. The means are available and will increase once the setbacks arising out of the Second World War are overcome. What is required is greater international collaboration in order to utilize to the full the facilities which already exist.

From this brief historical sketch of the growth of communications it will be appreciated that the degree of organization, economic, political and cultural, in the internal affairs of a State is largely dependent on the facilities for circulation which are available. Apart from the effects of international communications which will be discussed later, the function of internal circulation is to bind together the parts of the State in no uncertain manner. The validity of the geopolitical concept of the State as an organism is open to serious criticism in many of the deductions which its protagonists have made, but there is greater justification for the biological analogy in so far as the State's system of communications is comparable with the circulatory system without which life cannot be maintained in any organism. So commonplace are the means of circulation in advanced States that an attempt to draw attention to their importance may seem banal, yet the student of Political Geography must appreciate that their establishment, maintenance and improvement are essential to the activity and well-being of the State. No doubt societies could exist without well-organized systems of roads, railways, etc., as they have done in the past, but such communities could not claim to be States in the present-day meaning of the term and their people could scarcely rise above a mere subsistence level.

Furthermore, there can be no effective system of government without adequate means of communications, whatever the particular political régime may be. Centralization of political power, which to a great extent is a characteristic of all States, could never have been achieved without organized circulation. Here it is difficult to separate cause and effect. Attempts to concentrate political power in the seat of government preceded the construction of roads and railways, but once this internal policy was accepted, and when the building of communications had passed through an initial phase of meeting local or regional requirements, it was inevitable that, when lines of movement assumed a "national" pattern, they should reinforce the directive influence of both State and provincial headquarters. Governmental authorities, appreciating this unifying function of communications, then developed plans for the extension and improvement of communications, with the objective of still further centralizing the whole range of circulation activities so that the major route foci gained a new access of power.

This is not to suggest that internal communication systems were set up entirely for administrative purposes. Strategic and commercial considerations were probably of greater importance at first. In the case of railways and canals, the first stages of development were almost entirely concerned with local, commercial and industrial requirements, and it was not until well into the nineteenth century that anything approaching a complete national system of land communications appeared.[1] Yet the first decade of the twentieth century saw all well organized States in possession of at least the elements of a national network of roads and railways, frequently supplemented by inland waterways. The services provided by all these means of communication have been greatly augmented; the volume of traffic and mileage of routes have increased beyond anything reached in the past. In brief, internal circulation has

---

[1] The system of "Routes nationales" in France is an exception.

now reached a position of unprecedented importance in State organization.

So vital is its present role in national affairs that an increasing tendency towards "national" control is apparent. Even where communications are not directly administered by government departments, subsidies and other favourable treatment are frequently made available, with the result that internal circulation reflects national policy more and more directly. No single factor has made a greater contribution to the unification of States than this rapid expansion of circulation. Too seldom is it realized that nationalism together with the implementation of national sovereignty could not have reached their present stage without the concurrent growth of means of communication. That is one of the major reasons for the inclusion of a study of circulation in Political Geography. This does not imply that the technological progress of transport facilities should be investigated in detail, but it does mean that the carrying capacity, scope of services, distribution patterns and smooth running of means of communications constitute an essential element in the politico-geographical basis of every State.

Although the planning and construction of lines of communication reflect in no uncertain manner the ingenuity and skill of mankind yet two sets of conditions still exert a directive influence on internal patterns of movement. First, the physical factors of terrain and climate, while of less importance than formerly, cannot be said to have lost completely their effects on the development of communications. "Le climat est peut-être le seul adversaire qui ne soit pas de notre taille, le seul qui dépasse notre mesure humaine," says Capot-Rey,[1] yet the density and use of communications are still far greater on the plains than in the mountainous regions of the world. Marshes, rivers, forests, deserts and mountains have been conquered in the sense that routes have been constructed across or through them, but they still exercise a canalizing effect in so far as the makers of roads, railways and canals seek the easiest ways in overcoming these obstacles. Ease of movement on land is largely

[1] *Géographie de la Circulation sur les Continents*, Paris, 1946, p. 273.

a matter of gradient; hence the utilization of valleys and passes in mountainous areas.

Notwithstanding the engineering achievements of such countries as Switzerland, where roads and railways have been built for special purposes, the major arteries of movement follow the easiest gradients, and even in regions of lower elevation, a similar adaptation to terrain is discernible, while on the plains quite moderate interruptions of the relief are sufficient to cause deviations in lines of movement.

Again, as geographers and engineers are well aware, bridging points on rivers serve to focus routes at physically favourable places, and navigation limits on rivers are an expression of depth and volume of water. All these and many other physical conditions illustrate the influence which the terrain still exerts on the development of circulation and help to explain that perpetuation of the use of early lines of movement to which Capot-Rey refers.

But it must be admitted that, when allowance has been made for the directive influence of physical factors on the layout of communications, the second set of conditions is of greater importance. It consists of the economic and strategic requirements of the State which, either together or separately, have played a greater part in determining the internal pattern than any other group of conditions.

There is little point in discussing whether circulation preceded the route or *vice versa*. The initiation and development of both are so intimately interwoven, and reveal such a high degree of reciprocity, that they are inseparable. What is significant is that routes only become major arteries where there is sufficient traffic, either present or potential, to justify their maintenance and improvement. Clearly, densely populated regions, especially where they are highly industrialized, require a greater density of communications than sparsely inhabited lands which have less need of transport facilities.

Again, the character of the national economy affects a State's internal circulation. A country which is occupied mainly by peasants dependent on subsistence agriculture does not require such communications as are appropriate to a State wherein specialized agricultural methods and cash-crop farming make internal exchange of commodities essential. The greatest need of circulation is felt in those highly organized States, the successful continuance of which rests on the closest integration of industrial, agricultural and commercial activities giving sustenance to a dense population with high standards of living.[1] Thus Great Britain, France, Germany and the United States of America occupy outstanding positions in the world as the possessors of standards of circulation which mark them out as unified political entities and also contribute greatly to the material well-being of their inhabitants. It is therefore permissible to speak of the economic strategy of States in regard to internal communications and the policy behind that strategy aims at securing the maximum efficiency of movement.

At the same time, States are also concerned with military and political aspects of their communication systems although the emphasis laid on these aspects varies widely according to the objectives of the countries concerned, and is determined by external rather than internal considerations. In sum, one of the main functions of the State is to maintain circulation at its highest possible level and the successful fulfilment of this function calls for planning. As long as the State remains the primary political unit its existence as an entity depends largely on the extent to which its communications make possible not only the movement of commodities and people but also the interchange of ideas. It is difficult to avoid exaggeration when discussing the importance of the radio, telecommunications and the Press in this connection. They are all means of communications and their power to formulate public opinion, whether ill-informed or not, is a decisive factor in the evolution of national policies, in the development of national culture, and in the growth of that feeling of belonging together which marks off the people of one State from those of all others.

So far circulation has been considered from the point of view of the internal Political Geography of States, but, as Oppenheim reminded us, "The civilized States make a community of States because they are knit together through their common interests, and the manifold intercourse which serves

[1] The reader is referred to M. Jefferson, "The Civilizing Rails", *Economic Geography*, Vol. IV, 1928, pp. 217–231.

those interests."[1] That "intercourse" is made possible, fostered and augmented by various means of communications, but there is a fundamental difference between it and internal circulation inasmuch as the latter is free from external or foreign control, except in the cases of financial and technical assistance, whereas the former is now subject to the state of international relations and, indeed, is partly determined by international regulations.

There is also another important difference. Exception made of the circulation within the colonial empires, the great majority of internal movement is by means of land routes, including rivers, canals and coastal traffic. Against this, ". . . over three-quarters of the world's international trade, including the raw materials on which modern civilization so largely depends,"[2] are carried in ships using the oceans and seas of the world. Shipping is one of the oldest forms of transport; the seas and oceans which carry it are today the major links in the chain of global circulation of commodities and passengers. They are likely to continue this essential function in world communications in spite of the introduction of cables and wireless for the transmission of news and other information, and are therefore a prime geographical factor in international affairs. Perhaps the best illustrations of their world importance are provided by the fierce competition which has developed between rival maritime States, as well as between individual shipping companies, and by the sustained efforts of non-coastal States to acquire access to the sea. "One of the oustanding questions of the future is how far the subsidized uneconomic competition that has characterized the past can be averted without some degree of international planning under Government auspices."[3]

In addition to its importance as the greatest single medium of world trade and intercourse, oceanic circulation is characterized by certain features which differentiate it from movement on land.

In the first place, the oceanic waters, together with their bordering seas, are continuous; in effect, they constitute one

[1] L. Oppenheim, *International Law*, 5th edition, edited by H. Lauterpacht, London, 1937, p. 262.

[2] O. Mance, *International Sea Transport*, Oxford, 1945, p. 10.

[3] O. Mance, *op. cit.*, p. 11.

vast region of circulation which occupies nearly four-fifths of the earth's surface. "The ocean was one all the time," wrote Mackinder, "but the practical meaning of that great reality was not wholly understood until a few years ago—perhaps it is only now being grasped in its entirety."[1] Because of its continuity and the absence of formidable physical barriers, except in Polar regions, the ocean is in time of peace the great unifying factor in world communications. It provides accessibility as between high and low latitudes and between regions of disparate economy and culture, and is therefore of vital interest to all States, including those which have no frontage on its shores. It attracts trade and passengers to its ports to such an extent that the continental lines of communication are largely feeders to the oceanic circulation system. In this sense, the morphology of the oceans and the ease of movement on their waters determine the lineaments of the pattern of global communications. The ocean has ceased to separate the land-based States; it unites them in a way which is beyond the capacity of land routes.

The second distinguishing feature of oceanic communications arises out of the fact that shipping has been relatively free from the inhibiting political control which has hindered the development of international land communications. There are no demarcated political boundaries on the seas and, apart from agreements to use certain lanes, as on the North Atlantic, there are no legal restrictions as to the route a ship may follow. Once it is outside "territorial waters", its commander becomes almost a law unto himself; hence the great and sometimes awe-inspiring responsibility with which the captains of ocean-going ships are endowed.

This so-called freedom of the seas has no parallel on land nor in the air. Once the possibilities of ocean traffic were appreciated, it was inevitable that competition should develop so that national merchant marines grew rapidly and with far-reaching results. World-wide exchange of commodities, with all its effects on national economy and trade policies, was greatly stimulated, and economic interdependence on a global scale appeared for the first time. Colonial dependencies assumed a

[1] Mackinder, *op. cit.*, p. 29.

new importance for their mother countries, and certain small States, such as Norway and Greece, which are poorly endowed with internal material resources, were able to make great additions to their national revenues by acting as sea-carriers of the commodities and passengers of other States. All the great Powers, and many lesser States, sought to acquire an increasing share in this remunerative activity, with the result that world tonnage of vessels of a hundred tons and upwards increased by 50 per cent between 1913 and 1938, whilst some indication of the importance of shipping in war-time is given in the table compiled by J. S. Maclay which shows that the world's gross tonnage increased from 56.8 million tons in September, 1939, to 69.0 millions in September, 1945, in spite of the enormous war losses.[1]

This widespread attention to the development of merchant marines has had many repercussions in the policies of the States concerned. Various means have been tried in efforts to foster national shipping interests, ranging from the long-abandoned Navigation Laws of Tudor and Stuart times to the more recent attempts at discrimination which have been accompanied by State intervention in the form of subsidies for shipbuilding and scrapping, whilst some States have assumed direct control of their merchant fleets.

Justification of these policies has been made on the grounds of national security and economic necessity, but the result has been to increase the difficulties of international shipping relations, difficulties which can only be overcome by international co-operation. Such is the importance of oceanic communications to the world as a whole, that any threats to it arising from subsidy wars and other forms of uneconomic competition should be averted. This explains the growth of the Conference System[2] and requires a world-wide international organization to ensure that the freedom of the seas shall be able to confer the maximum benefits on mankind.

Up to the present time, circulation on the oceans has been

[1] J. S. Maclay, "The General Shipping Situation", *International Affairs*, Vol. xxii, No. 4, October 1946, p. 489.
[2] For details of international organizations for the control of shipping, *see* O. Mance, *op. cit.*

developed under national flags (with the exception of temporary wartime pooling arrangements) and each maritime State has endeavoured to safeguard the movements of its ships by the use of naval power. This action is necessary as long as international rivalry exists and gives rise to the possibility of interference, although piracy has disappeared. The result is seen in the building of great naval fleets, the sole function of which is to safeguard the use of the ocean highways. The measure of sea power is therefore the aggregate of merchant and naval vessels, the two elements serving the State in complementary style.

The third feature which characterizes oceanic traffic is the peculiar pattern into which its routes fall. Excluding for present purposes national coastal traffic and ferry services, the great maritime routes conform to three sets of what may rightly be described as geographical conditions.

Firstly, they link those densely populated regions of high material productivity which are lowlands with an oceanic frontage, such as the plains of North-west Europe, the great river basins of China and India, and the coastal plains of North and South America. These coastal lowlands act as regions of attraction for the exportable surpluses of interior continental areas and as regions of entry for commodities destined to interior markets. They are therefore the focal areas of world traffic. As they are relatively few in number, and as shipping shows a very strong tendency to use the large ports, with their better handling facilities, greater opportunities for cargoes, and generally more favourable insurance rates, the great bulk of oceanic circulation is concentrated on a comparatively small number of major routes, so that their terminal points acquire ever-increasing importance.

So far, this is a question of Economic Geography, but when it is realized that coastal lowlands are divided between independent States, and that the economic hinterlands of great ports are rarely restricted to the territory of a single State, it will be appreciated that this problem of oceanic circulation has a marked political aspect, in so far as it plays a part in determining the commercial and naval policies of the States concerned. Great Britain's interest in the neutrality of Belgium is not to be dissociated from its desire to see Antwerp remain free from the control of another Great Power; Italy's efforts to obtain Trieste and Fiume, and later to retain them, is closely connected with that State's policy of increasing its share of world trade; the so-called Treaty Ports could hardly continue as such once China could claim to be an organized political entity capable of making and implementing a commercial policy of its own.

In passing, it is worthy of note that the United States is the greatest single possessor of highly productive, densely populated coastal lowlands with easy, well-organized access to the interior. That this endowment is appreciated by its Government is suggested by its achievement of more than parity in naval power with its chief maritime rival, Great Britain, and by the fact that it has taken the place of Great Britain as the leading State in gross tonnage of merchant shipping.[1]

Secondly, if the economic, demographic and political conditions of the oceanic shorelands provide the driving force behind the development of oceanic routes, the physical characteristics of the oceans themselves play no uncertain part in the delineation of the paths which the ships follow. The barrier function of the ice-infested Polar regions restricts all but occasional traffic to the zone between 60° North and 60° South, and within this zone ocean circulation would probably have developed into three closed and separate systems, but for the open waters which connect Atlantic and Pacific to the south of South America, Atlantic and Indian Ocean at the Cape of Good Hope, and Pacific and Indian Ocean either through East Indian waters or to the south of Australia. The influence of these open waterways made possible that unification of oceanic circulation on which, more than any other single factor, world economic interdependence depends. For some centuries their utilization gave rise to the hegemony of

---

[1]

	1939	1945
United Kingdom	16.5	12.5 million tons.
United States	8.5	40.1 ,, ,,

J. S. Maclay, *op. cit.*, p. 489.

Western Europe in maritime trade and, perhaps more important, facilitated the spread of Western civilization with all its results, calculable and incalculable.

A further outstanding feature in the morphology of the oceans is that the major units approach each other very closely at two places in the latitudinal zone mentioned above. At Panama, the Atlantic and Pacific are near enough to have permitted canal construction and at Suez, the Mediterranean, which for purposes of world trade is an extension of the Atlantic, is separated from the Red Sea arm of the Indian Ocean only by the narrow Isthmus of the same name. The construction of these two interoceanic canals has led to a reorientation of the lines of movement of oceanic trade. The North Atlantic retains the greatest volume of traffic, but from it two axial lines now spring off; one westwards to tie Atlantic and Pacific circulation at Panama; another eastwards to link the trade of the Indian Ocean and some of that of the Western Pacific with the North Atlantic.

These man-made breaches in the land barriers to oceanic trade have had an immense effect on the direction and volume of world trade, as the statistics of canal traffic show;[1] to such an extent have they concentrated circulation at these two points that they have acquired world-wide significance, having long passed out of the range of merely Egyptian or Panamanian national policies. Their use and freedom of passage are important to all the States interested in sea trade and a good case can be made out for placing their control under an international authority.

The physical character of the oceans and their shorelands has a further bearing on the development and maintenance of maritime movement. For the satisfactory functioning of shipping, both of the mercantile marines and of naval vessels, a vast series of ancillary services is required. This ranges from fuelling and victualling bases, through repair and maintenance facilities, telecommunications and commercial organizations, to the latest development of meteorological services. Security from interruption must be maintained, particularly where world routes

[1] For statistical details *see* A. Siegfried, *Suez–Panama et les Routes Maritimes Mondiales*, Paris, 1945.

have to negotiate "narrows" and their approaches; hence the desire for strategic bases by all the great maritime States.

No example is more illustrative of the necessity of implementing a policy designed to secure freedom of passage than that followed by Great Britain. A widely-travelled French authority on international affairs has written: "On sait avec quelle intelligence, quelle persistence, quelle minutie, l'Angleterre s'est arrangée à en posséder tout un réseau."[1] The allocation to Australia and Japan of mandates over Pacific islands, after the First World War, the efforts of the U.S.S.R. to obtain bases in the Baltic and in the Straits, American and British interests in the Caribbean Sea, all point in the same direction. States concerned with the maintenance of maritime circulation pursue what may be called communications policies and, as far as ocean routes are concerned, those policies are directed by the physical conditions of the water masses, their shores and islands, and their outcome is clearly indicated on the political map of the world.

Thirdly, and arising out of a combination of the two previously discussed sets of conditions, the network of maritime routes occupies an extremely small fraction of the immense surface of the oceans. There is a far greater concentration of traffic on "main lines" than there is in continental traffic, and the oceanic network is much less dense than its counterpart on land. This is partly due to the fact that the unit of transport at sea, the ship, has a much greater carrying capacity than a train, a barge or a road vehicle,[2] but the primary cause lies in the physical nature of the uninhabited oceans; their function in world circulation is to connect, in the main, a relatively small number of inhabited land areas. Their services are direct, irrespective of local requirements. This directness reflects the absence of political boundaries and is guided by the availability of bases and the distribution of terminal points.

In view of all these considerations, no State can afford to

---

[1] *Ibid*, p. 3.
[2] It is also noteworthy that the size of ships has increased markedly. O. Mance, *op. cit.*, p. 172, gives the following figures:
1913, 30,591 ships totalling 46.97 million gross tons.
1930, 30,990 ,, ,, 67.8 ,, ,, ,,

ignore the effects of oceanic circulation on its political and economic structure. Even the U.S.S.R., the least favourably situated geographically of the Great Powers to share in international sea trade, has made strenuous efforts, under its present and its former régime, to acquire additional ocean outlets. Its policies in the Black Sea, in the Baltic, in the Arctic and in the Western Pacific all suggest that it is not only aware of the advantages of oceanic communications, but is determined to establish itself in a position at least comparable with its chief rivals. The outcome will be seen in clashes between the competing Powers—they have not been absent in the past—and the political problems of the Middle East in particular, where West European, Soviet and now American interests are in close rivalry, will provide interesting material for the political geographer.

Again, the struggle for access to the sea by non-oceanic States is a further illustration of the power of attraction of maritime circulation. Before the Barcelona Conference of 1921, shipowners in interior States were obliged to register their vessels at some foreign port under the foreign flag and subject to foreign mercantile law. The Barcelona Agreement, now accepted by some forty States, recognizes the rights of such countries to the possession of a national flag for shipping; facilities in free ports, or free zones of certain ports, together with through traffic facilities between their territories and foreign ports, have done much to compensate interior countries for their lack of oceanic shores.

Such arrangements are subject to inter-State agreement, and their successful implementation rests on the maintenance of good relations. In Europe several examples were provided by the treaties which were signed after the First World War. Czechoslovakia was granted free-zone facilities at Hamburg. Jugoslavia received similar treatment at Salonika and her acquisition of Sušak was intended to be a compensation for her failure to obtain Trieste and Fiume. Austria and Hungary— each became an inland State after 1918—were given special conditions on the railways serving these two ports.

Not all these political arrangements worked satisfactorily. Jugoslavia made practically no use of its free zone at Salonika but developed its other Adriatic ports, to the detriment of Sušak and Trieste. Poland, with facilities at Danzig, preferred to build and develop a new port at Gdynia. The granting of independence to Trieste and its immediately adjacent territory after the Second World War, even though special facilities be provided in the port for the States which comprise its hinterland, will not be successful unless good relations develop between the new Free State and Jugoslavia, because the latter controls its hinterland communications.

Such European examples tend to attract attention because of the political and economic repercussions which may occur as a result of their application, but it should not be forgotten that Bolivia's attempts to gain access to the sea have for long been a cause of dissension in South America. Africa, like South America, has only one independent inland State at present, Abyssinia, which has sought outlets to the sea through foreign territory. The Belgian Government made arrangements with the British Government for the use of a site in Dar-es-Salaam as an outlet for the trade of the Belgian Congo, and similar arrangements have been made for Northern Rhodesia and Nyasaland to use the port of Beira in Portuguese Mozambique. Clearly participation in oceanic circulation, whether favoured by ownership of densely populated, physically appropriate, coastal lowlands or where it necessitates complicated negotiations with neighbouring States to make possible access to tide water by inland countries, is of vital importance in the Political Geography of all but the most insignificant States.

In discussing circulation on the continents, the student of Political Geography is confronted with a very different set of conditions. "Freedom of the seas" has long been debated in connection with maritime international communications and "Freedom of the air" has become almost equally euphemistically used in recent years, but studies in the various aspects of international affairs, including circulation, are seldom if ever concerned with "Freedom of the lands". The reason is all too obvious. Land communications have been developed primarily to meet the requirements of the internal organization of the State, and have therefore borne a close relationship to national policy. Since all but island States are in physical contact with their neighbours, the various national networks of routes have gradually been linked together, and through services of many kinds have been provided; but the essential fact remains, that in each country the primary objective is to retain control of communications within the territory of the State so that international traffic becomes possible only as a result of mutual agreement on the part of the political entities concerned.

Each and every national network is potentially a closed system, and the growth of economic nationalism in the twentieth century has served to reinforce this character by the creation of artificial barriers at political boundaries. Furthermore, this nationalist quality of land communications has encouraged differences in technical aspects. Russia and the two Iberian countries adopted railway gauges different from that of the other European States. Rate structures and systems of administration are almost as numerous and as varied as the countries which possess them. In some States there is direct Government control of railways, while in others this form of transport is privately owned and directed. Where it is considered necessary, for economic security or for strategic reasons, transport services are subsidized directly or indirectly by favourable freight rates.

International land traffic is therefore hindered by being subject to the laws of the State through which it passes[1] and by difficulties connected with differences in technical equipment and administration. In view of these obstructive conditions, it is a matter for some surprise that international land circulation has reached its present high level which is an index of the efforts made by the organizers of international agreements in this field. Their work is subject to modification with every boundary change and with developments in the political ideologies of States.

---

[1] Most neighbouring States now have arrangements for the passage of goods "in transit" and usually in sealed vans. Such goods are usually not subject to customs inspection but they must figure on an agreed list of commodities. Such facilities do not exist for road traffic and rarely for goods transported on inland waterways.

Co-ordination of continental circulation is further hindered by the existence of a variety of forms of land transport. Whereas on the oceans all traffic is carried by ships, on the land, railways, roads and inland waterways are in competition with each other. Each received a great stimulus from the Industrial Revolution and its concomitant development in circulation, but each progressed independently of the others, making internal co-ordination difficult enough, as the conflict between rail and road interests in Great Britain shows.

Again, all three types of land transport are tied to fixed routes, the construction of which entails vast expenditure of labour, materials, and capital. They are not designed for the purposes of international circulation. Seldom do they follow the most direct international lines; they are frequently characterized by deviations to meet national interests. Land routes are therefore less flexible than those on the oceans; they are less easily changed, although the volume of traffic may fluctuate considerably. The result is seen in the greater density of means of circulation on the continents, more particularly in the industrialized regions of the more advanced States, but international intercourse is restricted to certain points where facilities for crossing political boundaries have been supplied.

Europe provides the outstanding example of a continent where this conflict between national and international circulation is still unsettled. Its highly organized economic activities and dependence on external sources for raw materials and markets suggest the desirability of the freest possible continental circulation, yet because of its political fragmentation that circulation is hindered by restrictions imposed for political reasons along every one of its fifteen thousand miles of State boundaries. The danger in such a system lies in the opportunities it provides for a powerful State to dominate smaller countries through its international trade.

In the past, Germany's policy, summarized in the phrase "*Drang nach osten*", was put into practice by commercial agreements which ultimately led to economic hegemony in Danubian and South-eastern Europe, as Basch has shown.[1]

[1] A. Basch, *The Danube Basin and the German Economic Sphere*, London, 1944.

During the inter-war period, Italy attempted a somewhat similar economic expansion with less justification and much less success. The U.S.S.R. is now implementing a similar policy in Eastern Europe and has already re-orientated the commercial relationships of that troubled region; Poland, Czechoslovakia, Hungary, Roumania and Bulgaria are being ever more closely geared to the Russian economic system. Inevitably such economic control in the affairs of other States is associated with increasing political influences so that Europe is split into two opposed camps.[1]

The political geographer will appreciate that one of the most important factors in the development of such policies is the existence of international circulation which, being subject to national control, can be used as a weapon for economic and political ends by States which so desire. In an ideal world, continental communications would be freed from all artificial obstructions so that they could exert a unifying influence comparable to that exercised in peace time by the great oceanic highways, but that cannot be achieved while sovereign States retain the power to restrict international movement to meet national ends. Here is another argument for the partial sacrifice of sovereign power by States.

All the available evidence points to the desirability of a rapid approach to the unification of global circulation. Land and sea transport are not competitors; they represent complementary elements in a world system. Soon after the First World War, Vidal de la Blache wrote:[2] "La dernière phase de l'histoire des communications est caractèrisée par l'intense collaboration du rail et de la navigation à vapeur." Since that date there has been a large increase in road construction and traffic, largely because of the extension of the use of the internal combustion engine, but this has had little effect on international circulation. In the main, road transport of goods is restricted to relatively short hauls and the tendency for such traffic is to feed the railways, which still remain the chief means for the carriage of goods on a continental scale.

[1] For further details see Chapters iii and viii in *The Changing World*, W. G. East and A. E. Moody (eds.), London, 1956.

[2] A. Basch, *The Danube Basin and the German Economic Sphere*, London, 1944, p. 258.

The major objective of further unification of world transport therefore rests on the closer integration of rail and sea traffic, but this is dependent on the removal, or at least the reduction, of tariffs which are undoubtedly the chief obstacle in the way of developing international trade. To what end has space been conquered and travel times reduced if the advantages gained by human ingenuity and skill cannot be utilized fully? This is more than a national question. Without adequate distribution, world production of commodities is fettered, and consumption levels are kept low. Those who would argue that this is no concern of the political geographer overlook the fact that the political structure of the State reflects the success or failure of the economic activities of its people.

Conversely, nothing delays economic development more than political instability and malaise.

> "Plus la civilization prend un caractère économique, plus la politique et l'économique sont entremêlées: plus aussi les moyens de circulation sont multiplés et perfectionnés, plus les faits de transplantation humaine liés à toute exploitation intensive de la terre deviennent d' abord nombreux et ensuite variés."

wrote Jean Brunhes.[1] In fine, circulation is one of the most important means by which world society functions as a going concern so that every obstacle to its successful working should be removed.

Railways and the motor-car are comparative newcomers to continental circulation, but rivers have served as highways since very early times. The hydrographic system of south-eastern England was exploited by the Saxon invaders of that territory; Russia was for long dependent on its rivers for transport purposes, and the great streams of the New World guided the penetration of that continent by European immigrants. But navigable rivers differ from their competitors as highways in so far as the lines of movement on their waterways are antecedent to the evolution of States in their modern form. All that man can do is to improve the river's navigability, raise its carrying

[1] *La Géographie Humaine*, Vol. I, p. 281, 4th edition, Paris, 1934.

capacity and extend its sphere of usefulness by connecting it to other rivers or the coast by canals.

Where a large river system is wholly contained in the territory of a single State it can be of great assistance to internal circulation, but where the navigable course is shared by two or more States traffic is subject to interference where there is no system of international control. Such a river will have little to contribute to external trade unless there is co-operative action among the riparian Powers to bring about improvements in navigability and uniformity of navigation regulations. Furthermore, the traffic on such a river is of interest not only to the States through which it flows, so that the fullest use of its navigational facilities is most likely to be made when the river is "internationalized", that is, when its control passes under a Commission set up by all the interested States. This procedure undoubtedly leads to some abrogation of the sovereignty of the riparian Powers, but the sacrifice is justified by the material benefits derived from the increased traffic on the waterway.

Europe, again because of its political fragmentation, has several rivers which fall into this category and the Danube was the first river to be internationalized. After the First World War, similar arrangements were made for the Rhine and the Elbe, but the smooth working of these Commissions, which were created to facilitate international circulation, was interrupted by political considerations, Germany being the worst offender in this regard.

In the future, as in the past, Europe will need the services of every possible means of continental transport, and international rivers can play their part. Their great advantage is their low freight rates; Capot-Rey cites the findings of a French inland navigation expert on the relative costs of inland transport, that by water being three times cheaper than that by rail and five times cheaper than by road.[1] Against this advantage must be put the much lower speeds of inland water transport. On the other hand, river barges are very appropriate to the carriage of bulky, non-perishable commodities such as coal, iron ore, oil,

[1] Capot–Rey, *op. cit.*, p. 211.

grain and timber, which are precisely the commodities in greatest demand in Europe.

Other systems of international circulation are also of interest to the political geographer inasmuch as they facilitate the smooth working of States and the more widespread distribution of resources of all kinds. An outstanding example of international co-operation is the Universal Postal Union. Founded in 1874, its Postal Convention states that all the countries of the Union, and only a few minor countries are not members, form a single postal territory for the reciprocal exchange of correspondence. The International Telecommunications Union has been less successful in its work of developing international co-operation because of the conflict with political interests, more particularly as regards wireless telegraphy. All the more important States possess their own internal radio systems which exert a powerful political influence, especially since the introduction of cheap receiving sets.

Although it is not yet possible to assess accurately the effects of wireless telegraphy, there can be no doubt that it has already become an important factor in international relations. The dissemination of news, political propaganda and what may be called cultural material through the new medium may go far to break down international misunderstanding. On the other hand, it has been used to foster nationalism and each State is anxious to secure wavelengths which suit its purposes. Without international agreement in the allocation of wavelengths there would be confusion "on the air", and to avoid this dilemma the International Telecommunications Union holds regular conferences to make decisions on the adjustment of wavelengths as well as other technical matters. It should also be remembered that telecommunications greatly assist the world-wide exchange of commodities, and thereby play their part in world production and distribution.

One of the dominating factors in the economy of every State is the availability of mechanical energy. The sources of this energy, coal, petroleum, running water, and now the materials from which atomic energy is derived, are notable for the unevenness of their distribution, so that material prosperity and the political power which is associated with it are largely dependent on the possession of, or access to, adequate supplies of one or more of these commodities. Hitherto, deficit States have met their requirements by the importation of coal or oil supplies through normal trade channels, but in order to safeguard supplies, increasing State interference has become common in what were originally commercial arrangements. Since 1918 the number of trade agreements between States has increased greatly. Sometimes they are incorporated in Treaties; failing this, they are usually sponsored and negotiated by the appropriate Government agencies, which means that international trade is increasingly directed to fit national policies. This is true of most of the commodities conveyed by international land and sea communications, but it is especially important in the case of fuels, because they, and the energy they generate, are basic factors in the development of industry and transport and, to a growing extent, of agriculture. Both coal and oil are also bulky commodities, and expensive to transport over long distances, even when source and market are favourably located with regard to cheap water communications.

Two twentieth century developments are capable of greatly easing the disadvantages of the world's uneven distribution of energy resources. The large scale generation of electricity, by the use of coal, oil, or running water, and improvements in the technique of long-distance transmission have led to the growth of national grid systems. In the United States, large areas are already served by a widespread grid, and in Europe the only apparent barriers to an international system of distribution over equally large areas are those associated with national boundaries. Electric power is already exported from various countries to neighbours which require it and three regional schemes were in operation before 1939: Norway and Sweden were transmitting electricity to Denmark, Bavaria's current requirements were partly met from hydro-electric stations in Austria, and a Franco-German scheme for the utilization of hydro-electricity, generated by the Rhine, was initiated under the Treaty of Versailles.

Technically there are no serious obstacles to the further extension of the grid system in an international field. Three-phase transmission is the commonest method employed in

Europe and variations in voltages can be overcome by trans-
former stations. The advantages to be gained are certainly
great. Mance[1] points to the benefits to be derived

> " . . . by balancing sources of water power which reach
> their maximum in summer with those attaining their
> maximum in winter, by marrying the coal and water power
> supplies to the best advantage and possibly to some extent,
> by staggering the peak load as a result of the variation in
> time over a widely extended area."

German experts formulated international schemes for
Central Europe during the interwar years, and a Polish
geographer has suggested how the States of East Central Europe
could be electrified by a combination of thermal power from the
Silesian coalfield and hydro-electricity from the Danube,
circulated by an international grid. Such schemes and their
extension to wider areas cannot be put into full operation until
the appropriate States are ready to grant powers to an international body.

Somewhat similar to the transmission of electricity is the
circulation of liquids and gases by pipelines. Again the United
States has developed a network of such lines for the distribution
of petroleum and natural gas. In Europe, valuable experience
was gained during the Second World War when extensive pipelines were laid in England and between this country and France.
The pioneer experiment in international pipelines was the
connection of the Kirkuk oilfield in Iraq to the eastern shore
of the Mediterranean. To meet political and strategic requirements, it was decided to bifurcate the line at Haditha, the
northern branch terminating at Tripoli and the southern at
Haifa, and the necessary agreements for the crossing of Syria
and Lebanon as well as Transjordan and Palestine were com-
pleted between the Iraq Petroleum Company and the French
and British authorities as the Mandatory Powers of the
territories concerned.

In spite of the disturbing political conditions in the Middle

[1] O. Mance, *International Road Transport, Postal, Electricity and Miscel-
laneous Questions*, London, 1947, p. 140.

East since the opening of these pipelines in 1934, the experiment has been sufficiently successful to justify the preparation of another scheme to link the Persian Gulf oilfield with the Mediterranean in spite of the location of this field near a sea coast. Such projects are undoubtedly beneficial to the distribution of oil and gas, and the creation of international pipelines together with continental electricity grids would lead to greater ease of circulation of mechanical energy, to more even spread of industries, to greater mechanization of agriculture and consequently to a greater productiveness, without which political stability is unlikely to be achieved in the less well-endowed parts of the world.

There remains to be considered the place of air transport in international circulation. This, the latest and most rapid means of communication, is a twentieth century development, and has brought into external State relations a new element which is so young and has grown so rapidly that it is impossible to calculate with any accuracy its short and long term effects. Many forecasts have been attempted; not all of them have been untainted with gross exaggeration.

The aeroplane, in one form or another, must certainly be recognized as a medium of both internal and external communication, but it seems unlikely to be able to compete successfully with other means of transport for the carriage of goods because of its large operating costs. J. S. Maclay gives another shipping expert, Mr. Leslie Runciman, authority for the statement that

" . . . one moderate sized cargo vessel in a single peace-time year carried three times as much freight measured in ton miles as the whole of the highly organized domestic air lines of the United States; secondly, that the cost per ton mile by air was about 30d. while the similar cost for the ship before the war was about one-thirtieth of a penny."[1]

Air transport will certainly compete for the carriage of special commodities, of small bulk and high value, and has already proved to be of importance in carrying cargoes to places

[1] J. S. Maclay, op. cit., p. 490.

E

which are inaccessible by other means. Its main field in peace-time is concerned with passenger transport, to which it brings great advantages in speed if not in costs.

An outstanding geographical feature of air communication is that it brings to movement over land that element of directness which is characteristic of shipping routes. There are dangers in flying over mountainous regions, and atmospheric disturbances frequently cause aeroplanes to be diverted from normal courses, either in a vertical or a horizontal direction. Otherwise, air traffic is capable of following the shortest routes between its landing places, the location of which determines the pattern of airways. Yet aerodromes are not dispersed along Great Circles, even when they serve long-distance international traffic, and for two reasons.

As with all other forms of transport, air services develop largely in response to demand, actual or potential, and demand for the regular supply of this expensive means of travel is generally restricted to routes between densely populated, highly produc-tive regions.

Secondly, international air traffic involves flying over the territory of States other than that in which the aircraft is owned, unless uneconomic deviations are to be made. This gives rise to the possibility of infringement of the sovereign rights of the States over which the flight is made and has led to prolonged debates on the "Freedom of the Air".

"After forty years of discussion, the nations of the world have not yet agreed on any universal rule as to the privileges which the aircraft of one nation should enjoy of flying over or landing for refuelling or commercial trading purposes in foreign territory."[1]

In practice, and in legal theory, the right of all States to control the air space, *usque ad coelum*, and extending to the limits of territorial waters, is generally recognized. This makes the State a three-dimensional entity and, as far as aircraft is concerned, international routes can be worked only by consent of the States over which commercial aeroplanes fly. Hence a powerful weapon is put in the hands of States, more especially

[1] J. C. Cooper, "Some Historic Phases of British International Civil Aviation Policy", *International Affairs*, Vol. XXIII, No. 2, April 1947, p. 189.

those which lie between regions most likely to develop air communications, because they are in a position to force aircraft to follow other than the most convenient routes.

For some years British air routes between the home country and India and Australia were not permitted to cross Italian or Persian territory. Before the Second World War, air services between London and Nigeria were routed via Cairo and Khartoum because of the monopoly of Air France in the French Sahara, and thereby lengthened the journey by over 2,800 kilometres.[1] In the outcome, the formation and use of air routes were largely determined by reciprocal arrangements between States or, as Cooper says, "Straight political bargaining was accepted as the rule to be followed"[2] during the interwar period. Here again is evidence of the conflict between political interests, inherent in the existence of a large number of sovereign States, and the full development of aerial circulation as indicated by an analysis of geographical conditions.

Efforts have been made recently to resolve some of the difficulties associated with this conflict. The Chicago Conference on International Civil Aviation of late 1944 proposed international agreement on "Five Freedoms": freedom to fly across the territory of contracting States without landing, freedom to land for non-traffic purposes such as refuelling, freedom to land and take up, respectively, traffic between a State running an air service and any other State party to the agreement, and freedom to pick up and set down traffic between States on the route of an international air service. Mainly because of the opposition in the policies of the United Kingdom and the United States (the U.S.S.R. was not represented at the Conference), the negotiations broke down and the earlier bilateral system was continued. In 1946 the United Kingdom and the United States, the most important States engaged in international air traffic, signed the Bermuda Agreement, but this was a bilateral document, and although it may pave the way for more extensive international agreement, its provisions are at present restricted to Anglo-American civil aviation.

In view of the terribly destructive character of aerial warfare

[1] *Vide* Capot-Rey, *op. cit.*, p. 272.
[2] J. C. Cooper, *op. cit.*, p. 196.

combined with the ability of aircraft to carry war into the heart of enemy territory, the fundamental problem of international air traffic is that of national security *versus* free aviation. State policy in this connection must be governed by the judgments of military and aviation experts. The political geographer recognizes in this, as in many other aspects of world circulation, the obstructive nature of national policies where designed to meet the exigencies of potential warfare.

In sum, the physical character of the earth's surface, the distribution of land and sea masses, the all-embracing nature of the atmosphere, together with the uneven distribution of population masses and economic productivity, point the way towards the goal of integrated global circulation. Paradoxically enough, this universalism has been and still is opposed by the particularism of individual States. The chief political problem of the twentieth century is to reconcile these opposites, and the number of international conferences which have been held since the opening of the century is indicative of the awareness of most States of at least its existence.

VII

DEMOGRAPHIC ASPECTS

In Chapters I and II emphasis was laid on the triune character of all States each of which is an amalgam of territory, people and the organizational machinery which is set up to guide the relationships between people and their physical environment. This chapter is devoted to an analysis of some geographical aspects of the demographic element within the State, and in its external relations. It is hardly necessary to elaborate here the importance of this element in State and inter-State activities, but the student of Demographic Geography should be warned of the great complexity of this subject.

In the present state of knowledge, adequate statistical data are not available for over half the world's population, and the census material of even the most advanced countries does not fully meet the requirements of demographers. Moreover, population problems are related to a wide range of contributory causes, biological, social, economic, political and psychological, none of which are strictly geographical, but all of which must be recognized in evaluating the demographic structure of the State. This, of course, is only another way of expressing the well-known fact that human relationships are more complex than those of all other organisms, and that man is the only form of life which has attempted political organization.

In common with that of the areas and of the economic and political developments of States, the distributional pattern of the world's population is characterized by marked unevenness both in total numbers and in density. This irregularity is not a direct expression of mere area whether continents or States are considered as the territorial units. Although Professor Fawcett[1] has shown in his simplified diagrammatic representations of land areas and their populations that there is a broad correlation between these two geographical elements, a decisive

---

[1] C. B. Fawcett, *The Bases of a World Commonwealth*, London, 1941, Figs. 5 and 6, pp. 28-29.

factor is that continental populations are themselves very unevenly spread as a result mainly of the existence of differential capacities to support people. Nevertheless, there is a striking concentration of population in Asia and Europe which has been continuously maintained for the last three hundred years. According to the calculations of Sir Alexander Carr-Saunders,[1] Asia and Europe together contained 78.9 per cent of the world's population of 545 millions in 1650 and 79.7 per cent of the 2,057 millions in 1933. Europe alone, and in spite of its comparatively small area, has increased its proportion of world population from 18.3 per cent in 1650 to 25.2 per cent in 1933, although there was a steady drain on its numbers due to emigration throughout the nineteenth century and during the first two decades of the twentieth.

There is also great disparity between States in area and population. Even the Great Powers are very dissimilar in this regard, as Professor East has shown,[2] and, for various reasons to be discussed later, there is unlikely to be any equalization of population numbers among States in the future. Hence, the political geographer is confronted by a set of demographic conditions, the import of which may cause him to ponder seriously, yet there can be no doubt that such conditions are of primary significance in both the internal and external affairs of States.

Neither a large total population nor a high density of human occupancy alone is enough to give a State major political importance. People are necessary to cultivate the fields, to man the industries, and so forth. They are in many respects the chief resource of every State, yet a high level of economic productivity is not necessarily a corollary of dense population. Witness the example of China, which is reputed to have the largest coal reserves in the world and undoubtedly possesses the largest population, yet it has not become an important industrial country.

To achieve political power in the world, quantity of population is of less importance than its quality, the latter

---

[1] A. M. Carr-Saunders, *World Population*, Oxford, 1936, Fig. 8, p. 42.
[2] W. G. East, "The Nature of Political Geography", *Politica*, Vol. II, No. 7, March 1937, p. 273.

finding its expression in the will to win and maintain a leading position in international affairs. Admittedly, a thinly peopled State of low total population has little or no opportunity of becoming a Great Power. There may be an optimum population in relation to the stage of development and the total resources of the State, but there does not appear to be any similar optimum for success in the struggle for hegemony in world affairs. The leading States of the present time, U.S.S.R., U.S.A., Great Britain and France, reveal marked divergences in numbers and density. No country has wielded more influence in the world and for a longer period than Great Britain, yet its total population has never exceeded fifty millions. This number would be inadequate to utilize fully a territory the size of that of the U.S.S.R. or U.S.A.

Clearly, from the point of view of competing for a place among the leading Powers, each State is unique in its endowment of terrain, material resources, geographical location and population. Its chief distinguishing human feature is the will combined with the ability, that is, the quality, of its people, and this represents a combination of biological and psychological attributes concerning which there are practically no statistical data. Our views on the quality of both our co-nationals and of other peoples are all too frequently coloured by prejudices. This emotional attitude, all the more powerful because it is usually not fully conscious, is undoubtedly inimical to a rational and peaceful settlement of international population problems. Its existence should be recognized by the political geographer if only because it provides at least part of the explanation of the means by which the leaders of certain States have been able to win the support of their people in expansionist activities.

Another important feature of demographic conditions is that population numbers fluctuate for reasons that are not always clear or ascertainable. Looking first at the world as a whole, its human inhabitants have shown an "unprecedented expansion"[1] in modern times or, to be more precise, between 1650 and 1933, and the termination of this process is not yet in

[1] Carr–Saunders, *op. cit.*, p. 42.

sight. The rate of increase has not been constant, neither for the world nor for its component parts, but the absolute increase from 545 millions in 1650 to 2,057 millions in 1933 presents the greatest single international problem of the present day because there is a direct relationship between the needs of these millions of people and the productive capacity of the earth's surface. That relationship is most clearly reflected in the enormous gap which now exists between actual food production and the amounts required to bring the consumption levels of a very large proportion of the world's people to satisfactory standards. This gap can no longer be bridged, if it ever could have been, by national organization. "There is far from true world sufficiency of any biologically produced material, whether for food or industry, if we hold total need as our criterion."[1]

Clearly, international planning is necessary to deal with this colossal and urgent deficiency of foodstuffs, and that not necessarily from any altruistic motive. The material self-interests of all States are directly involved, since even the wealthiest Powers, U.S.A. and U.S.S.R., are not able to supply all the requirements of all their people satisfactorily and the less well-endowed countries are still more dependent on production outside their own territories.

Furthermore, the basis of international trade rests on widespread demands for food and other commodities. If these demands are to be met, even with the present low standards of living prevalent over large areas, an expanding world economy is required together with a collateral improvement in distribution. The United Nations Food and Agriculture Organization, which sprang out of an international conference at Hot Springs in 1943, is a step in the right direction and has made very valuable suggestions for dealing with the problem, but its schemes will not achieve full success unless and until all the producing and consuming States conform to a commonly accepted food policy. "Freedom from want" must remain a euphemism for the greater part of the world's increasing population until food production and distribution are radically

[1] G. C. L. Bertram, "Population Trends and the World's Resources", *Geographical Journal*, Vol. cvii, Nos. 5 and 6, May–June 1946, p. 193.

reorganized. Until that change is brought about, population pressure, on the territory of individual States and against national boundaries, will remain a powerful motivating force in world affairs. As long as its effects, including the policies it gives rise to, are canalized in unilateral directions, the major problem will remain unsolved.

A further complicating factor in the manifold problems arising out of a rapidly increasing world population is to be found in the uneven distribution of rates of reproduction, excluding for the moment the effects of migrations. Natural increase of population is the result of excess of births over deaths, and on this basis the world's population is still increasing, largely because of improvements in medical science and in social conditions and the elimination of famine from large areas where it was previously endemic. The outstanding fact here is the difference between Europe, and the European derivatives, and the rest of the world.

"The rapid population growth of Europe," wrote Notestein,[1] "is at an end. Demographically speaking, Europe has reached maturity. . . . For two centuries Europe and Europe overseas have had dynamic, growing populations in a comparatively slowly changing world; European populations are now approaching population stability in a rapidly expanding world."

The period of marked increase in European population began soon after 1700, but the time of most rapid expansion was the nineteenth century. At present, the excess of births over deaths is still sufficient to show some increase in absolute numbers, but population "projections" indicate a considerable falling off in the near future. More important from the demographic point of view is the changing age structure of the population in West European countries where, as a result of a combination of decreasing reproduction and increased expectation of life, there is temporarily a large proportion of

[1] F. W. Notestein and others, *The Future Population of Europe and the Soviet Union*, Geneva, 1944, p. 69. The reader is referred to the diagrams and maps in this valuable work.

people in the higher age groups. With the death of these older groups, the full effects of decreasing fertility will be experienced since the net reproduction rate[1] is not high enough to ensure replacement of the population. Holland and Eire are the only two countries of North-west Europe with a net reproduction rate above unity. By contrast, the States of Mediterranean Europe (excluding France) and of Eastern Europe (excluding Czechoslovakia but including the Soviet Union) all show rates above unity, although there is evidence that fertility is already decreasing even there. In brief, the population of nearly all Western Europe and most of Central Europe is not replacing itself while that of the rest of the continent is only doing so at a decreasing rate.

The consequence of these population trends in Europe is that its north-western countries have ageing populations which are not being replaced, whereas the eastern and southern States are occupied by still growing populations, with greater fertility and a higher proportion of young people. The political implications in this differentiation are manifold and have given rise to population policies in certain countries. These have been directed towards increasing fertility; they have been experimental and have been too recently implemented to allow judgment of their success or failure. "We should also realize that political questions may play a far more important part than economic questions in influencing decisions (in population policies)",[2] wrote D. V. Glass, and his view was certainly correct in the cases of Germany, Italy and France. Political geographers will appreciate the relation between demographic structures and European affairs which is suggested by Notestein's map of the distribution of net reproduction rates in this part of the world.[3]

Elsewhere in the world, excluding those countries which have been settled and developed by peoples of European origin, the areas with large and dense populations, such as China, Japan,

[1] For details of the methods of calculating reproduction rates, see D. V. Glass, *Population Policies and Movements in Europe*, Oxford, 1940, pp. 383–7.

[2] D. V. Glass, *op. cit.*, p. 368.

[3] F. W. Notestein, *op. cit.*, Fig. 1, p. 18. Reproduced, with minor modifications, in Fig. 6, on opposite page.

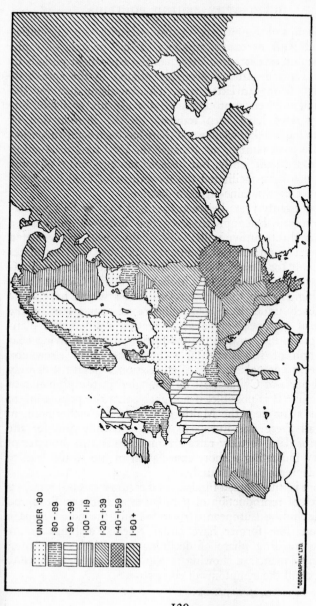

UNDER ·80
·80 - ·89
·90 - ·99
1·00 - 1·19
1·20 - 1·39
1·40 - 1·59
1·60 +

'GEOGRAPHIA' LTD.

Fig. 6

Distribution of Net Production Rates in Europe about 1930–35. Based on Notestein "The Future Population of Europe and the Soviet Union", Geneva 1944

India, Java and Egypt, are confronted with the difficulties associated with excessive numbers. Their periods of rapid population expansion came later than the equivalent periods in Western Europe and are probably related to the spread of knowledge from the latter area. The requisite data for the calculation of their reproduction rates are not available, but mortality rates have been reduced by the introduction of European medical knowledge and there has been some reduction in the effects of famine, not because the total food production has increased sufficiently, but because modern means of communications have facilitated the movement of food into what would have been famine-stricken districts.

In the twenty years between 1921 and 1941 India's population increased by approximately one hundred millions, a phenomenal rate of five millions per annum even when related to the 1921 population of about 320 millions. Only estimates are available for China, and these usually place its total population above that of India. It is probable that the Chinese death rate is higher than that in those countries which have come more closely under European influence as is suggested by the absence of European-organized irrigation systems and plantation agriculture, so that the proportion of people living near the margin of subsistence may be higher than elsewhere. Whatever the actual numbers of population, at least the densely peopled parts of China must be entangled in the problems of congestion. "It is possible, if not likely, that the population of China is at or near the Malthusian limit."[1] Furthermore, in nearly all these non-European lands, and allowing for the absence of data, fertility rates are high, otherwise the rates of mortality indicating a short expectation of life would lead to a large decrease in total numbers.

There is, therefore, a fundamental contrast in both numbers and rates of reproduction of population as between European lands, including European derivatives, and the non-European countries. The former have either reached stability or are entering the first phase of declining population; the latter, excluding Japan, are showing no signs of decreasing fertility yet reveal all the symptoms of congestion.

[1] Carr–Saunders, *op. cit.*, p. 290.

Here the political geographer is faced with a dilemma of the first order and one which he shares with all students of international affairs. On humanitarian grounds, the millions of under-nourished Indians, Chinese, etc., are entitled to adequate diets and to the benefits of improved health services; on economic grounds, the predominantly agricultural populations of these congested countries might well justify a general raising of their standards of living by providing expanded markets for the highly industrialized countries.

Given these three advantages, infant and adult mortality rates would almost certainly decrease rapidly, reproduction and expectation of life would increase and the various populations would expand enormously. This is what happened in western Europe during the nineteenth century, but note the difference. At that time Europe was not congested, developing industries were absorbing increasing numbers and there were outlets for surplus population on the other side of the Atlantic. Now, in the middle of the twentieth century, at least South-east Asia is already heavily populated, and emigration is almost completely barred; in any case, the means of transport available for emigration purposes is totally inadequate for the volume of traffic which would be necessary to do more than scratch at the surface of the problem.

Industrialization has begun in Japan, India, and to a less extent in China, but their domestic markets are restricted by the prevailingly low purchasing capacity which characterizes these countries. Simultaneously, nationalism has started to make rapid strides so that there will soon be demands for the Asiatic equivalent of *"lebensraum"*, and with more justification than the claims of National Socialist Germany.

The long-term solution to this complex problem may come by methods similar to those employed in Western Europe, by the voluntary limitation of the size of families associated with the extension of birth control, but the immediate dilemma remains. Whether the optimists, who predict that a solution will be found by a process of more or less rapid adjustment, are more correct in their forecasts than the pessimists, who used to declare that the world was faced with a "Yellow Peril", there is no doubt that a new force has entered the arena of world affairs.

Owen Lattimore, who has spent many years in Asia and is a
very competent observer, wrote:

> "It is the importance of Asia which makes this war a
> watershed. Asia was for several centuries an area in which
> political history and the economic fate of hundreds of
> millions of people were determined by things that happened
> somewhere outside of Asia. We have now crossed over into
> a period in which things happening in Asia, opinions formed
> in Asia, and decisions made in Asia, will largely determine
> the course of events elsewhere in the world."[1]

An important point for the political geographer is that
population pressure in Asia has become chronic at a time when
large areas of the earth's surface, particularly those under
European control but outside that continent, are undeveloped
or, at best, underdeveloped. Further, the internal organizations
of India, China, Indonesia, Japan, Burma, Siam and Indo-
China are simultaneously passing through a phase of critical
change. As Professor Fleure[2] reminds us:

> " . . . the traditionalist life necessitates a minimum of
> large-scale organization, and the peoples of these lands
> have been very helpless in face of more highly organized
> outsiders, even when weapons only indirectly came into
> consideration. The Chinese in the nineteenth century were
> described as the least governed civilized people in the
> world."

The devastating civil wars in China, the Indonesian demand
for political independence, the resistance encountered by the
French authorities in their Asiatic territories and the newly-
acquired dominion status of India and Pakistan are visible
evidence of the wishes of Asiatic peoples to find their own
political salvation. These changes, concerning as they do over
half the world's population, may result in transformations of
national economic and political structures, but there will remain

[1] O. Lattimore, *Solution in Asia*, London, 1945, p. i.
[2] H. J. Fleure, *Some Problems of Society and Environment*, London, 1947, p. 9.

the problem of population pressure as a formidable element in world affairs.

Before States assumed their present form, each enclosed by a rigid boundary, excessive population had no immediate political repercussions. Where satisfactory adjustment between population numbers and material resources was not achieved by birth and mortality rates, migration was the normal procedure, either within restricted areas or on a continental scale, the best example of the latter type being that of the emigration of Central Asiatic peoples which led to the Barbarian Invasions of Europe in the early centuries of the Christian Era. In the twentieth century, only two kinds of migratory movement are possible. Within States, migration is politically unhampered—it may be officially encouraged—but between States, immigration is subject to the laws of the receiving country, and in some cases emigration is expressly forbidden or officially discouraged. No amount of migration will alter the world's total population at any given time, but the very existence of States has established barriers to free human movement, and has therefore abolished the possibility of relieving pressure even if adequate means of transport were available.

This imposition of restrictions on migration is a very recent development. It has been estimated that during the period 1846—1932 over fifty million European migrants crossed the Atlantic in a westerly direction.[1] The stream reached a peak in the decade which preceded the outbreak of the First World War, but the post-war movement dropped rapidly, mainly because of the introduction of the quota system in the United States. During the same period there was relatively little intercontinental movement of non-European peoples, partly because of the lack of transport facilities available to these poverty-stricken masses, but mainly because of fear of the real or imagined effects of the acceptance of large numbers of Asiatics and others on the economic, political and cultural organization of the States to which they might have migrated. Inter-continental population movements have therefore reached a very low ebb. The overcrowded lands can expect no relief in their

---

[1] Carr–Saunders, *op. cit.*, p. 49.

struggles against congestion from the more sparsely inhabited countries. In consequence, there will be, sooner or later, a recrudescence of the rivalry between "Have" and "Have-not" States and, possibly, an intensification of nationalism unless the individual States find other solutions to their population problems.

Having briefly discussed some of the salient features of world population, attention may now be directed to those internal problems which are related to the numbers, densities and trends of population. Clearly the size and composition of its population are of primary importance to the State, but it is only in recent years that serious attention has been paid to national demographic structure; in consequence, the development of population policies is at a very early stage. The most advanced States have compiled census statistics for a comparatively short time and a large percentage of the world's people have never been enumerated. In the absence of reliable data, population planning was quite impossible, but it is interesting to note that, when information did become available in Western Europe, its uses were first directed to social and economic changes, as the Malthusian interpretation of demographic conditions shows.

It was not until the beginning of the twentieth century that the political importance of population was appreciated to such an extent that it found its application in the formulation of population policies, and the first States to take such steps were those suffering not from expanding populations, but from actual or imminent decline in numbers. The fundamental problem here is the maintenance of a balance between population, on the one hand, and the resources and requirements of the State, both domestic and external, on the other, and this is true whether the philosophical considerations which underlie government policy are primarily concerned with the interests of the individual or with those of the State as a whole. In other words, there is an optimum population for each country,[1] but because of the great diversity between States this optimum is peculiar to each of them and in no case does it hold good for

[1] For a detailed discussion of the population optimum, see A Landry, *Traité de Démographie*, Paris, 1945, pp. 567–588.

very long periods because of changes which inevitably take place in the population itself as well as in the national resources, the utilization of the latter being particularly subject to the influence of technological developments.

For these reasons, and for lack of sufficiently detailed demographic knowledge, it is difficult, if not impossible, to calculate precise numbers for the population optimum of a State, but efforts to achieve the state of equilibrium which it implies are obviously necessary if the bad effects of congestion or of inadequate replacement rates are to be avoided. The stage has not yet been reached when exact population "targets" can be set nor is there sufficient agreement among demographers as to the best methods of reaching the optimum. A great deal of research is still necessary before national policies can be evolved and applied successfully over a considerable length of time. France, Germany, Italy and the Scandinavian countries have been pioneers in efforts to adjust their human numbers to State requirements,[1] but their motives as well as their methods have varied considerably. Family allowances, income tax concessions for married people, the amounts sometimes increasing with the number of children below certain ages, legislation against abortion and official discouragement of birth control, encouragement of earlier marriages and appeals to parents to increase the size of their families for patriotic reasons, are among the methods which have been tried to arrest population decline, but no considerable reversals of trends have become observable; indeed, most of the steps taken so far appear to be mere palliatives. They may be summed up in the words of a well-known British demographer: "However urgently governments may have declared their desire to increase the supply of births, they have nevertheless persistently tried to buy babies at bargain prices."[2]

If national population policies have not been notably successful so far, they have drawn attention to the value of demographic knowledge to the State. Internal organization is dependent on the availability of man-power to meet the many

[1] D. V. Glass, Chapters III to VII of *Population Policies and Movements*, gives full accounts of the population policies of these countries.
[2] D. V. Glass, *op. cit.*, p. 371.

needs of the State, and this human element represents something more than the total number which results from the excess of births over deaths. In those countries which have a rapidly increasing population there is no anxiety about a deficiency of man-power; their problem is to find sufficient employment for their inhabitants. But in countries where the net reproduction rate is at or below unity, there is often an actual or potential shortage of labour which may well cause alarm. Such is the present position in the United Kingdom as well as in other Western European States. Temporary alleviation may be found in the increased employment of female labour and in the stepping up of output per man hour, but these stop-gaps are not unlimited in their efficacy, so that "direction" of labour may become an important part of economic planning.

This raises a number of political and social problems, more particularly in the highly industrialized countries where fluctuations in domestic and foreign markets suggest that an increased mobility of labour is desirable. During the Second World War, Germany was forced to organize large-scale transfers of population and tried to maintain her level of production by the compulsory "direction" of millions of "slave labourers" by methods which would be unacceptable in peace time. To rehabilitate her economic position, Great Britain is re-introducing the wartime expedient of "direction", while France, in spite of having pursued a population policy for longer than any other State, has for some years been compelled to encourage immigration as a means of bolstering up her declining national labour force.

Such government-controlled modifications of the occupational distribution of population are indications of the departures in State organization from the haphazard conditions which were associated with *laissez faire* in the nineteenth century. In Europe, including the U.S.S.R., planned economies are gradually involving the planned distribution of the population, as well as attempts to control its demographic structure. They are the means by which some States are adapting their social, economic and political institutions to changes in population conditions. They are among the phenomena which political geographers are bound to consider in their analysis of the State's internal affairs.

In addition to the relationships between economic and social conditions and population, there is also the effect of the military requirements of the State to be considered. The threat of war, in some form or other, has never been absent from the world and seems unlikely to be in the near future. From this point of view, States fall into two categories, those which are actually or potentially aggressive and those which are or may be subject to the aggression of others, but, in each case, a proportion of national resources, including population, is devoted to the armed forces and, it should be noted, the prestige of the State is often measured in terms of military power. This means that a varying percentage of the man-power of every State is withdrawn from directly productive work, more particularly during times of international tension. Where a State, such as Britain or France, has overseas commitments and at the same time is failing to replace its domestic population, the clash between economic and military demands for man-power becomes acute. Some relief may be found in the employment of "native" troops where these are available, but the bulk of the forces are recruited from the population in the home country.

Quite apart from actual warfare, which has its own peculiar effects on population trends, the peace-time maintenance of armies, navies and air forces causes a steady drain on the population in just those age groups from which they can least conveniently be spared. Furthermore, the labour engaged in armament industries of all kinds is not occupied in directly productive employment in the strictly economic sense unless the products are exported for sale. At the time of writing, Britain is passing through a severe economic crisis, in part due to shortage of labour, but is maintaining armed forces and auxiliary services which absorb over a million people. The following table, which has been compiled from an official publication,[1] illustrates the position in this country, which can hardly be described as an aggressive State:

---

[1] *Economic Survey for 1947.* Command 7046. H.M.S.O., February 1947, Table A, p. 33.

Distribution of Total Man-power in Great Britain.

	1939 June Thous.	1945 June Thous.	1946 June Thous.	1946 Dec. Thous.	1947 Dec. Thous.
Total in Civil Employment ..	18,000	16,416	17,415	18,122	18,400
Armed Forces and Auxiliary Services	480	5,090	2,032	1,427	1,170
Total in Employment	18,480	21,506	19,447	19,549	19,570
Demobilized Men and Women not yet in Employment	—	40	700	300	100
Insured Unemployed	1,270	103	376	398	400
Total Working Population	19,750	21,649	20,523	20,247	20,070

In this table, man-power is defined as including males aged 14—64 years and females aged 14—59, and it will be seen that in December 1947 over 5 per cent of this man-power was engaged in non-productive employment. Here it should be pointed out that Britain's present position is a special case in view of its large-scale commitments arising out of its status as a World Power and out of its successful participation in the Second World War, but this does not lighten the task of those statesmen who are responsible for the allocation of labour.

France provides another example of the effects of military requirements. Since her defeat in the Franco-Prussian War of 1870–71 fear of further German invasion has dominated her population policy. In consequence, France has freely recruited coloured troops into her armed forces and has become the chief country of immigration in Europe. Between 1851 and 1931, the numbers and percentages of aliens in France rose steadily from 375,289 (1.06 per cent) to 2,891,168 (6.91 per cent), but even these figures do not give a complete picture of the number of immigrants since many aliens become naturalized.[1] Carr-Saunders[2] reports the results of an enquiry which

[1] Carr–Saunders, *op. cit.*, p. 154.
[2] *Ibid*, p. 158.

was held in 1928–29 and which showed that 47 per cent of all workers in mines and quarries in France were aliens and that in cement works, chemical works, public works, contracting, and sugar refineries over 40 per cent were aliens. "The French are, in fact, abandoning heavy work to foreigners, and this is the basis of the complaint that is sometimes heard in foreign countries that the French are building up a new form of slave state."[1]

Against this criticism should be placed the treaties and similar arrangements made by France with other European countries, notably Poland, whereby the conditions of work, rates of pay and contracts of immigrants are safeguarded. In many respects, France may be said to have treated her new-comers in a way which other States might well copy.

The economic, social and military factors which influence the demographic structure of the State undoubtedly play a vital role in its internal affairs, but there is another aspect of population which interests particularly the political geographer and that is the geographical distribution of this human element. Just as the population of the world is very unevenly distributed, so is that of every State. In general terms, disparity in population density is a function of the capacity of land to support its human occupants, but the numerical relationship between a given area and its inhabitants is subject to change. The physical conditions of geological structure, relief, climate and vege-tation are partial determinants of this capacity, as is the size of the political unit concerned, but the human response to the opportunities which they provide is also conditioned by modes of life, as expressed in political, social and economic organi-zation, and by technological developments.

Again, "support" of population is open to various inter-pretations which, in their turn, are mainly based on the pre-vailing standards of living in an area. There can be, therefore, no permanent optimum of density or total size, so that the terms "underpopulation" and "overpopulation" can only have validity when related to the circumstances at a given time. In consequence, density of population, as expressed in numbers

[1] *Ibid* p. 158.

per unit area, has little meaning unless it is associated with the capacity, organization and standards of living which obtain in a State, and this criticism is even more cogent where "average densities" over large areas are concerned.

" . . . we need research and experiment on modes of expression of densities; averages are as misleading as usual, and efforts to make population-contour maps have revealed the limitations of the idea."

wrote Professor Fleure.[1]

Some improvement in cartographic representation of population data is obtained by the dot method, but the inherent weakness in this system, as in that using isopleths, derives from the fact that census enumerations are based on administrative divisions and the boundaries of these territorial units, even of the smallest of them, rarely coincide with the limits of equally densely peopled areas. While admitting, therefore, that the distribution of population map of a State is one of the best guides to an interpretation of the demographic aspects of its political geography, it is also necessary to urge caution in accepting what it purports to show.

In practice, the spatial distribution of population within the boundaries of a State is determined by the possibilities of finding remunerative occupation together with desirable social amenities. From this point of view, the two major economic occupations of mankind, agriculture and industry, exert opposite effects on population distribution. The former is conducive to a relatively even spread of the people who practise it and depend on it, although the resultant spatial propinquity varies widely according to the type of farming and its associated economy. Peasant farming, as in parts of China, India and Eastern Europe, and irrigation agriculture, as in Egypt and the Punjab, may give rise to high densities; cash-crop production, especially where it is mechanized, usually directly supports much lower densities, and animal grazing areas, such as parts of Australia, New Zealand and North America, rank as thinly populated lands.

[1] *Op. cit.*, p. 6.

On the other hand, industrial occupations are characteristically associated with human agglomerations. In highly industrialized States, the strong tendency is for population to be concentrated in the areas of production of raw materials, more particularly of mechanical power, and, although this locating factor is losing some of its importance because of the rapid growth of circulation, the developed coalfields still rank among the world's most densely populated regions. The pattern of distribution of population therefore reflects the degree of emphasis which is placed on one or the other of these two human activities. Of course, there are no States which are solely concerned with industrial occupations, and even those countries in which agriculture employs the great proportion of the people have some industries. Moreover, all the major States include areas which for various reasons are inappropriate to either farming or industrial development, but the densely inhabited regions which, on any count, are the most important parts of States owe their population patterns to the type of occupation which predominates within them.

The advent of large-scale industries has not been an unmixed blessing in this connection, especially in those States of North-western Europe where they have replaced agriculture as the chief means of subsistence. They have greatly relieved the pressure of population—many observers advocate increasing industrialization as the only means of easing the problems of congestion—and they have been responsible for a great increase in material wealth. They have also caused changes in the distribution of people, largely through concentration in towns which ". . . has been marked by a disastrous harvest of slums, sickness, stunted population and human misery from which the nation suffered in mid-Victorian years and continues, though fortunately to a much less extent, to suffer today".[1] Rapid urbanization has been an accompaniment of industrialization in every State where this form of employment has been developed and is a demographic phenomenon which has thrust itself upon the notice of statesmen and geographers among many others. States with economies and political ideologies as diverse as those

---

[1] *Report of the Royal Commission on the Distribution of the Industrial Population.* Command 6153. H.M.S.O., 1940, p. 8.

of Great Britain, the U.S.S.R. and the U.S.A. have this much in common, that the "Drift to the Towns" has caused important modifications in the distributional patterns of their populations.

Great Britain occupies an unusual position for two main reasons. As the seat of origin of the Industrial Revolution, it was the first country to experience rapid and uncontrolled urban growth and this feature has not yet been checked. In its seven great conurbations[1] live nearly half of the total population. Greater London alone had an estimated total of 8,655,000 or 18.8 per cent of the population of Great Britain in 1937. It was the first city in the world to reach the million mark; in 1801, the year of the first British census, it had over a million inhabitants which represented 10.6 per cent of Great Britain's people, and this proportion has steadily increased during the following 140 years. The remaining conurbations, like London, have all increased at more than the average rate for the whole country which means that there must have been movement of people into these great agglomerations.

This concentration in large cities with its attendant sprawl of buildings has more serious repercussions in Britain than in many countries because of its comparatively small size. The Registrar General's estimate of Great Britain's population in 1937 was forty-six millions in an area of 88,750 square miles, giving an average density of 518 per square mile. (Similar figures for England alone were 38,552,000 in 50,330 square miles with an average density of 766 per square mile.) No national area in the world, except that of Belgium, which has only eight-and-a quarter millions of people, is so densely populated, and the continued growth of urban areas has meant encroachment on valuable land, millions of acres of which have passed out of cultivation.

In times when foreign produced food could be imported easily and cheaply, such sterilization of agricultural land for housing and industrial development caused no serious general concern, but since the end of the First World War, Britain's

[1] Greater London, Greater Manchester, Greater Birmingham, Merseyside, Glasgow, West Yorks and Tyneside: cf. C. B. Fawcett, "The Distribution of the Urban Population in Great Britain in 1931", *Geographical Journal*, Vol. LXXIX, 1932.

financial and economic situation has deteriorated to such an extent that more food must be produced at home and the fringes of the great cities should be preserved for agricultural purposes. For these two reasons, among others, Britain has set up a Ministry of Town and Country Planning which is entrusted with the task of reconciling the various claims to land in this densely populated, relatively small, country.

The U.S.S.R., in area, size of population and internal economic and political organization, provides a marked contrast with Great Britain, yet its population distribution also reveals a distinct growth of urbanization.

> "The rapid growth of cities in all parts of the U.S.S.R. has been the outstanding and controlling factor in the redistribution of population under the Soviets. . . . It will be noted that cities characterized by extremely rapid growth are found both in the older European centres, especially around Moscow and in the Ukraine, and in new, previously undeveloped regions."[1]

In the intercensal period 1926–1939 the numbers of cities over the 200,000 mark increased from 12 to 39 and at the end of that time they contained 13,557,000 people, a figure 90 per cent above their combined population in 1926. Some of these agglomerations developed with amazing speed; they were true mushroom towns Chelyabinsk's 1939 population expressed as a percentage of its total inhabitants in 1926 was 460.5 per cent, that of Alma Ata was 507.8 per cent and that of Novosibirsk was 337.6 per cent, but an even better index of the development of urbanization is that there were 174 towns of over 50,000 population in 1939, and of these 49 showed a threefold or greater increase between 1926 and 1939. The greater part of all these urban increases was due to migration from rural areas whereby some 23 millions left the country for the towns and constituted at least two-fifths of the Soviet urban population in 1939. Rapid urbanization came later in the Soviet Union than in Great Britain, but the causes were similar. In referring to the recent

[1] F. Lorimer, *The Population of the Soviet Union*, Geneva, 1946, p. 145.

growth of cities in the former State, Lorimer says: "This is, of course, an expression of the rapid expansion of industry, commerce and services."[1]

Turning to the Western Hemisphere, Lorimer calculates that "the land area within the January 1939 boundaries of the U.S.S.R. (8,176,000 square miles) is practically equal to that of Central and North America excluding the Caribbean Islands and Greenland" and that "the population of the Soviet Union at the beginning of 1939 (170,467,000 persons) was equal to 100.5 per cent of the population of Central and North America (same area)".[2] In the U.S.A. alone there were 137 million people living on an area of 3,738,000 square miles. During the period which ended with the close of the First World War the U.S.A. population pattern was largely determined by two factors, the steady movement of people westwards and the unique inflow of immigrants from Europe. In the early part of the third decade of the nineteenth century these two movements had almost ceased, just at the time that a rapid decline in the national birthrate began, but a third type of migration was already well established and reached a peak between 1920 and 1930. During that decade, according to O. E. Baker,[3] "city-ward migration amounted to approximately 5,000,000 and 86 per cent of the nation's increase of population was urban". While this number is both absolutely and relatively smaller than the 23 million Soviet people who moved to cities (in a slightly longer period), it must be remembered that the U.S.A. was far ahead of the U.S.S.R. in industrialization and urbanization before 1920.

These three examples indicate quite clearly that urbanization as a demographic phenomenon and thus a geographical "reality", with its many and varied implications, is independent of the size of State territory and, so far, of any particular political régime. That it is closely associated with the rapid growth of industrial and ancillary activities is equally

[1] *Ibid*, p. 145.
[2] *Ibid*, p. 1.
[3] O. E. Baker, "Rural-urban Migration and the National Welfare", *Annals of the American Association of Geographers*, Vol. XXIII, No. 2, June 1933, pp. 60–61.

beyond doubt. Corroborative evidence of this last statement is supplied by the relatively low percentage of urban population in such densely crowded but primarily agricultural countries as China and India, in both of which the village rather than the town is the typical social unit. "The modern rise of Calcutta, Bombay and Madras has been described as turning India inside out" and "Looking at China . . . here again, we have evidence of the 'turning inside out' ".[1]

Most of the very great cities of the Far East reflect the impact of European influence, through trade and administration. The tradition of living in towns is very ancient there, as it is in the Mediterranean Lands, but the urban function was to satisfy the needs of defence, regional agricultural marketing and the administration of potentates and, as such, did not give rise to excessive urban concentration of people. The conclusion is inevitable; in the words of the Royal Commission previously mentioned, ". . . it is in Europe and those countries of the New World that have been colonized from Europe that 80 per cent of these million-mark cities are still to be found, and it is in Western civilization and particularly in Great Britain that the modern development of urbanization has secured its chief hold".[2]

The many social and economic effects of urbanization which arise out of its modifications of the geographical distribution of population are too complex to be discussed here, but two considerations may be mentioned. First, the rapid developments of aerial warfare, including the use of atomic bombs, make large cities the most vulnerable targets and may revolutionize the strategic policies of States and their international relations. As far as can be judged, no towns in the world are beyond the range of the new weapons, the destructive capacity of which is indicated by the effects of the bomb which was dropped on Hiroshima. Second, the problems of over-concentration of population in urban areas have become so serious in many countries that planning of the distribution of population seems to be the only remedy. This is a new idea in

[1] H. J. Fleure, *op. cit.*, p. 16.
[2] *Report of the Royal Commission on the Distribution of the Industrial Population*, 1940, p. 12.

the organization of the internal affairs of States, and will undoubtedly evoke much opposition. The attractive power of very large cities is very great. Wider choice of employment, and fuller educational, medical and entertainment services, are among the many facilities which large towns can offer to their inhabitants.

So great is the "pull" that living in vast agglomerations, in spite of its not inconsiderable disadvantages, appears to have become the accepted mode of life for the majority of people in Europe and the States which it has founded overseas. Any attempts to redistribute population must be related to these considerations, if they are to be successful. Probably the most satisfactory solution will be found by the institution of planning regions, at any rate for the smaller States such as Great Britain.[1]

Once agreement is reached on the delimitation of these regions, and this will be no mean achievement, there will immediately develop the further problems of responsibility and the machinery of planning. On the political level, these may cause a major revision of electoral representation and will call for agreement on the division of power between the central and the regional authorities, and in this connection it is worth recalling that what may be done with comparative ease under a totalitarian régime usually takes more time and greater effort in a democracy. Against this should be placed the fact that the greatest single experiment in regional planning, that conducted under the Tennessee Valley Authority in the U.S.A., was designed and successfully implemented in a country the inhabitants of which take pride in their "rugged individuality".

So far attention has been directed to urbanization from the angle of over-concentration and its associated problems, but there are other aspects of towns which the political geographer will not overlook. The habit of living in cities is as old as civilization itself, as the evidence of Egypt, Babylonia, China and India indicates, and organized States cannot permanently

[1] On this point the reader is referred to "Discussion of the Geographical Aspects of Regional Planning", *Geographical Journal*, Vol. xcix, No. 2, February 1942; "Practical Regionalism in England and Wales", by E. W. Gilbert, *Geographical Journal*, Vol. xciv, No. 1, July 1939; *The Provinces of England*, by C. B. Fawcett, London, 1919; and *The Regions of Germany*, by R. E. Dickinson, London, 1945.

survive as such without their "nerve centres"; hence the intensive bombing of London, Berlin, Warsaw, Belgrade, etc., during the Second World War.

Towns grow and function for a variety of reasons. In their development they assimilate and express the economic, social and political activities of the areas which they serve. By a process of crystallization of the modes of life, needs and desires of the people of their dependent areas, they come to epitomize regional differentiation. There is diversity of interests, not only between town and country but between town and town, and as these elements are essential parts of the fabric of the State to which they belong, the ideal of unity in diversity can only be attained by a reconciliation of these interests on an equitable basis. In highly urbanized States, the town dwellers exert a powerful influence in national and regional affairs if only because of their numerical superiority. Consequently the States of the so-called Western World as well as those of Eastern Europe, including the Soviet Union, tend to be dominated by urban interests. That this is not entirely a modern phenomenon is suggested by the philological origin of the word "politics", but the dominance of urban communities in the affairs of independent political entities is more marked now than it was previously because of the existence of means of circulation on a greater scale. This cleavage of interests is particularly notable in democratic countries because, among other reasons, the voting power of towns greatly exceeds that of rural areas, so that there is often a lack of balance in the community as a whole.

The towns which particularly interest the political geographer are those from which large-scale organizational activities are carried out. These capitals, national, regional and local, the last in the sense of being the headquarters of local government, are keypoints in the structure of the State. In common with all towns, they have a functional character, and although theirs is rarely exclusively restricted to administrative affairs, it serves to place them in a different category from other urban agglomerations.

Two geographical factors have been largely responsible for the location of the capital cities of unitary States, all of which have grown from nuclear or core areas. First, then, the capital is almost invariably situated in the original nucleus of the State. Where there has been amalgamation of previously independent territories, the core of the successful unit has usually become the locus of the capital of the united territory. London, Paris, Moscow, Peiping are examples of this type, but the rule, if it be such, is not always followed. Modern Italy was unified under the House of Savoy, which derived its power and authority from Piedmont, but Rome was selected as the capital of the Italian State for historical and political reasons. Second, the satisfactory functioning of the capital rests largely on the degree of accessibility which it possesses. Granted that accessibility can be created by artificial means, for example, by the building of railways and roads and by the establishment of airways, most of the older capitals had achieved their political status before these adjuncts to accessibility were widely available. Indeed, the common practice among States has been to select the capital first and then to focus communication systems on it, that is, a site which had already demonstrated its accessibility was chosen and then its advantages of geographical location were enhanced artificially.

Accessibility, however, should not be confused with mathematical centrality. Few, if any, States have expanded evenly in all directions from their original nuclei, so that capitals are usually ex-centrically placed with regard to the territory as a whole—in some cases, this ex-centricity is emphasized as a result of a "forward policy" on the part of the State in establishing its headquarters towards the spearhead of expansion.[1] This was the case in Tsarist Russia when the former capital was shifted to St. Petersburg, but the Soviet Government showed a greater appreciation of both political geography and tradition in moving the capital back to Moscow.

Where tradition, regarded in this case as the persistence of the authority of the nuclear region, and maximum accessibility act in concert, capital cities are most likely to retain their status even when the productive capacity and population of areas within the State have changed. London was the capital of

[1] Cf. V. Cornish, *The Great Capitals*, London, 1923.

England long before the Industrial Revolution took place, but no threat to change its function has been suggested. Similarly with other States, unless political changes, induced by external or internal circumstances, override the existing considerations. Thus Poland has had four capitals; India and China have changed their capitals several times. Furthermore, when a city has been selected to act as the political focus of a State, no efforts are spared to enhance its prestige, partly to impress foreign visitors, but also to pander to the exhibitionist tendencies which the people of all States seem to possess. In no small degree, therefore, the capital city reflects the wealth, power and political organization of the State of which it is the administrative centre.

In the case of Federal States, the "national" capital falls into a sub-category of capital cities. Federation, whether as an association of previously independent and autonomous States, as in the U.S.A., or of former dependencies of another State, as in the Dominions of Canada and Australia, entails the incorporation of the pre-existent societies, together with their capitals, in the new entity which, itself, must have a seat of Federal Government. To locate this capital in an existing town would cause ill-feeling between the constituent elements in the federation. The U.S.A. and Australia have overcome this difficulty by allocating small areas in which the federal capitals have been built. Known as the District of Columbia and Federal Territory respectively, they have a degree of autonomy comparable with that of the older divisions of the federation. In each case, the capital is a new city concerned above all else with the administration of federal affairs and, as such, they are unlike the capitals of unitary States.

The Dominion of Canada chose a different expedient in locating its federal capital. While Ottawa is in Ontario, it is on the right bank of the River Ottawa, which is the boundary between Ontario and Quebec, the original Upper and Lower Canada, which were the two most important provinces at the time of federation. It is also closely related to the boundary between French- and English-speaking Canada, so that its position is as nearly neutral as possible. Examination of the appropriate population maps will show that all three of these capitals are located towards the edge of the most densely populated regions in their States. Like most State capitals, therefore, they have ex-centric positions, but they have been made accessible by road, air, rail and telecommunications.

Regional capitals are the focal points of areas within States which possess some kind of unity of their own. Confusion as to the meaning of the term "region" is caused by the practice of government departments in grouping together administrative areas and calling the results regions. For example, in the U.S.A., the Census Regions are arbitrary amalgamations of States for the purposes of the Statistical Bureau of the Federal Government. In Great Britain, the Civil Defence Regions which were constituted in February 1939, were designed to meet the exigencies of the war, which was then imminent, and were based on the county system of administration. As with States themselves, such "regions" rarely coincide with geographical regions, but, unfortunately, there is little agreement among geographers as to the exact boundaries of the latter divisions.

Further confusion arises, therefore, from the plethora of regions of various kinds, but, without going further into the vexed question of regional boundaries, it is generally agreed that each State contains a number of areas, each of which is differentiated from the remainder of the national territory by its unitary character, which may be the result of one or more of a number of determinants. Each of these regions, with the exception of those which consist of sparsely inhabited land, includes an urban area which acts as the regional metropolis. Commonly such towns are the headquarters of local government, but difficulties frequently arise as a result of the non-coincidence of administrative and regional boundaries. They are the regional foci of "services" of all kinds, educational, commercial, professional, transport; often they are the ecclesiastical, judicial and social centres and invariably they contain the offices and works of the regional Press. In a word, they crystallize and express the "life" of the region. Newcastle, Leeds, Manchester and Birmingham are English examples of the larger type of regional capital, while Norwich, Exeter, Gloucester and Oxford are on a smaller scale; all States provide similar examples, varying in size, character and function according to the regions which they serve. They all possess one common geographical characteristic: they are all nodal points. Their precise locations may have been decided by some local consideration of defence or convenience, but their success as capitals depends largely on accessibility from all parts of their regions.

In Britain and elsewhere the suggestion has often been made that a reorganization of governmental administration on a regional basis would be a worthwhile reform. National Socialist Germany experimented with the formation of *"gaue"*; in France, the *"départements"* replaced an earlier system of provinces and the institution of "Provinces" in England has been suggested.[1] Changes in the population pattern and in the economic activities of its people, as well as political and territorial modifications in the State itself, have resulted in the outmoding of earlier administrative arrangements. But whatever regions may be devised to meet present-day requirements, the existence of regional capitals should be considered. Their integrating influence is already established; they are well-recognized as the focal points of areas which may be ill-defined, but the limits of which can be determined by research.

Since the final word in any such schemes rests with the central authority, there is always the danger that over-emphasis will be laid on the convenience of administrators. This depends, in part, on the degree of accessibility to and from the selected capital, but geographers will continue to urge that a region should represent a synthesis of all its components, physical and human, and of these accessibility is only one, however much it may represent the interaction of the others.

Existing administrative areas rarely possess this regional quality. In most cases they were created and delimited to meet the demands of a political structure which has now changed almost beyond recognition. In England, for example, population shifts and alterations of the electoral system have made the county boundaries anachronistic, but County Councils commonly have their headquarters still in the old "county towns", which have therefore retained their status as local government capitals even though they may have been surpassed

[1] *See* C. B. Fawcett, *Provinces of England*, London, 1919.

F

in size and importance by other urban centres in the same county. The inevitable result has been that the newer towns have demanded and obtained autonomy as far as their local government is concerned, with consequent overlap and duplication of powers which have led to considerable dissension.

In some regions, compromise has been attempted by the creation of Joint Planning Authorities and in all counties there has been a more or less equitable sharing of administrative responsibilities between the County Council and the smaller Urban District and Rural District Councils. Such a piecemeal system, composed of several types of unit, all varying widely in size, population and economy, is inimical to any form of nationally conceived planning however much it may be justified on the grounds of conformity with local interests and tradition. If a balanced structure, both in the State as a whole and within its parts, is to be evolved, many of the present anomalies associated with the established boundaries of administrative units will have to disappear. One of the most probable results will be the enhanced importance of regional capitals to the detriment of at least some of the older centres of local government.

VIII

SUMMARY AND CONCLUSIONS

"Le sujet . . . est dangereux pour un savant, car il est tout pénétré de passions politiques, tout encombré d'arrière-pensées".[1]

IN their original context, these words referred to the Geography of Frontiers, but they apply with equal force to the larger subject of Political Geography. They indicate the necessity for objectivity in all its branches and they do not exonerate the political geographer who takes into impartial consideration those subjective elements in the make-up of all States which may and do arise from one or all of ignorance, tradition and the inherent weaknesses, moral and political, of mankind. After discussing the basic ideas of German Geopolitics, including the concept of the State as an organism, as a rational being, like a man with life and a soul, another famous French geographer wrote:

"Cette comparaison détruit la base même de la géographie politique puisque, par définition, l'État n'est pas un homme, mais une groupement d'hommes dont les lois d'existence ne sont pas simples, car elles se déterminent à la fois par sa localisation géographique, par son type d'économie et de civilisation, par des relations passées et présentes avec les groupements voisines."[2]

These "laws of existence" of human beings are in a category by themselves. They are closely related to the physical environments in which man lives—of that there can be no doubt—but environments are of many kinds and it does not necessarily follow that the adaptations of groups of people will be similar

[1] A. Siegfried, in the preface to J. Ancel, *La Géographie des Frontières*, Paris, 1938, p. vii.
[2] A. Demangeon, *op. cit.*, p. 24.

F*

even when the lands they inhabit are alike. Certain biological laws are universally applicable—if a man does not eat he will certainly die, and if his diet is seriously deficient in the appropriate quantities of essential food elements he will not enjoy good health—but no such clearly-defined and well-known laws have been discovered and applied to the relationships between States.

To a very great extent, each State is a law unto itself because the people of each are constantly endeavouring to adjust their modes of existence to the conditions indicated by Demangeon. That is why the world, in spite of its planetary physical unity, is split up into a large number of political entities, and in spite of the efforts of jurists to formulate and codify "international law", their findings are not yet universally accepted. Many States subscribe to various international agreements but until there is a global acceptance of the "rule of law" on a commonly agreed basis, international relations will be conditioned by compromise which usually finds its expression in political bargaining. This is the vital factor in present-day world affairs. The political geographer is forced to recognize its existence, for it determines, more than any other single factor, both the relationships between States and, to a less extent, their internal organizations. Peace may well be one and indivisible but, politically and economically, the world is very much divided, and, it may be added, divided against itself. This political fragmentation of a physically united whole is the great anomaly in world affairs, but it appears to have escaped popular notice. It is certainly a "reality" for the political geographer who sees its repercussions influencing policy-making in both direct and indirect ways.

So complicated and intangible are the forces at work that they are not reducible to fixed laws. There are certain common measures within groups of States, but these are ill-defined, arising as they do out of subjective rather than objective conditions. Any branch of study, therefore, which is primarily concerned with States and their relationships cannot be an exact science. The techniques of investigation of international and domestic affairs are not comparable with those of the scientist's laboratory; problems of relationships cannot be brought into the dissecting-room, nor are they capable of systematic classification. Much of the methodology of Political Geography is, therefore, of an empirical nature. Where orderliness does not exist, no amount of scientific examination will produce it, but, by the use of analysis and synthesis, which are typical of modern geographical methods, the nature of world disorder may be revealed, and that appears to be the first prerequisite to the establishment of world order.

The State represents the results of human efforts to bring order out of chaos in a restricted area. Demangeon was right when he said that many writers exaggerate the influence of "natural conditions" on political formations, and underestimate the contribution of man himself. The physical habitats of societies remain relatively static; man is the dynamic element. He is primarily responsible for the changes which have been stressed repeatedly in preceding chapters, and one of his greatest achievements is the persistent effort he has made to extend the domain of orderliness. His motives have not been free from self-interest; his methods have rarely been beyond reproach. All too often has force been invoked in the subjugation of peoples whose organization was inadequate to resist successfully their would-be rulers. The imperialism of many States has not been, and is not now, above criticism on humanitarian grounds, but no one will deny that progress has been made in the extension of orderliness in spite of the two catastrophic reversions to barbarism which have shaken the world in one generation.

It is highly significant that in the twentieth century, for the first time in history, attempts have been made to devise and establish a world order. Two of them may be dismissed as ill-judged efforts to impose military conquest on the world; their chief value to human welfare is that they have been the immediate cause of mankind's awakening consciousness of the fact that a new world order based on the free association of States is not only desirable but necessary. That awareness is a new feature of world affairs; it implies increasing political consciousness and justifies some hope that harmony may come out of the existing disharmony.

The reasons for the failure of the League of Nations, as the first attempt to create a unified world system by consent, are not easily assessed, but it should not be forgotten that many of its activities, such as the care of certain national minorities, were successful in that they marked a step forward in international relations. Its successor, the United Nations Organization,[1] inherits the results of these valuable achievements but finds itself confronted with the same kind of obstacles as those which hindered the work of the earlier League. Of them all, the most serious, because the most obstructive, are those arising from the existence of independent States which are unwilling to sacrifice any of their sovereign powers. The task of U.N.O., reduced to its simplest essentials, is that of finding a *modus operandi* for the resolution of the conflict between national interests and those of the world at large. The members of the Assembly and of its subordinate bodies have undertaken the greatest experiment in organization ever known. Their decisions will affect the welfare of humanity throughout the world, and because of this it is imperative that they should have all the available knowledge at their disposal, and by no means the least important branch of that knowledge is that of the adaptations of peoples to their physical environments within the territories of States, together with the relationships between them.

This represents the contribution which Political Geography can make to the evolution of a new world order. It is all too obvious that those "political passions" and "*arrière-pensées*" are precipitating clashes in the debates of U.N.O. which are characteristic of domestic as well as of international politics. The political geographer is concerned with the geographical realities, the "circumstance of place", the pattern and form of States and their modes of life, all of which are deeply rooted factors in human existence. His aim is to investigate and assess these conditions of living, but he may justly claim that the knowledge produced by his researches is of value in arriving

---

[1] The change in title is significant; Organization implies a world system based on close integration. There have been many Leagues of States, but their subscribing members have always retained independence of action.

at conclusions concerning the nature of world order and unity.

In the past, expansion, with or without the assistance of armed force, was the normal procedure followed in attempts to correct the disharmonious patterns of men and things. The twentieth century has already seen experiments directed towards finding a new way of bringing about harmony in the world. They are based on the replacement of unilateral territorial expansion by universal co-operation, but, it may be pointed out, harmony cannot be established between unknown quantities. As Professor Taylor urged at the Dundee meeting of the British Association for the Advancement of Science, "The precise assessment of the geographies of the United States and the Union of Soviet Socialist Republics becomes as important as the precise understanding of their ideologies."[1] Her argument is all the more cogent because the two States named are indubitably the most influential Powers in the world, but knowledge of the geographical basis of the structure of all States also ranks among the essential prerequisites to the building of a new order.

These claims for more and more geographical knowledge rest on the following considerations. All States represent the organized attempts of their peoples to adapt their manifold activities to the physical conditions of their environments. Of the latter, there is a great variety, and similar types do not necessarily evoke like responses, nor do the relationships between physical *milieu* and its inhabitants remain static; they change from time to time. In consequence, the earth's surface is occupied by a wide assortment of societies, each with its own characteristics and interests, but quite apart from any rigid theories of geographical determinism or of mere possibilism, there is a close relationship between each society and its territory. For reasons which have been explained in previous pages, all the habitable parts of the globe are now incorporated in States, all in contact with each other, sometimes by direct contiguity, sometimes by intermingling of interests.

In a very real sense, therefore, there is a world society, but

[1] Reported in *The Times* of August 29th, 1947.

because of the tremendous centrifugal force of national separatism that society has not been able to assume the form of a world State with its attributes of a common system of government, of law, of economic organization. Each State is a part of this global community, not yet in a formalized system, but as a going concern. Precise assessments of the geographies of these separate States indicate the folly of trying to impose uniformity on these disparate units. Unity in diversity is the ideal; order without rigid, sterile uniformity is the catalyst in the synthesizing process of global integration, but synthesis must be preceded by analysis. No single line of investigation can supply all the answers to all the questions which will arise, but his holistic approach and specialized techniques make the contribution of the political geographer worthy of consideration.

Three illustrations, selected from the many available, may serve to throw light on the interests and methods of political geographers in studying world problems. First, the good geographer, like the good soldier, develops "an eye for country". If he is primarily a geomorphologist, his interest is in land forms, but if he is an exponent of that branch of the subject with which this book is concerned his vision will range over wider areas and will regard the earth's surface as the locus of political States. If he is able to enlarge his vision by extensive travel he will observe that the "cultural landscapes" are modified by human action, and that, for example, the pattern of land use may change as abruptly as it does when the Russian–Polish boundary of 1939 is crossed.

This is but one of many changes associated with the crossing of national boundaries which summarize the differences in character between adjacent States. Where the disparities between conditions on opposite sides of a political dividing line are pronounced, there tension may be expected, so that the adjacent margins of incompatible but neighbouring States are zones of strain. Such areas are frontiers in the geographical sense. They may be coveted by the interested Powers for strategic, ethnic or purely economic reasons; their disposition in the past has been settled by warfare, but today they are the subject of debate at international conferences. Upper

Silesia,[1] Alsace,[2] the Julian Region at the head of the Adriatic,[3] are typical examples of these maladjustments between States, and the political geographer, knowing that the disease exists, looks for the symptoms. By library studies and field investigations, he analyses all the aspects of the case and seeks to discover causes for its existence as a running sore in the body politic.

Unfortunately, a sufficient number of case histories of this type has not been compiled, but then, Political Geography is a young subject, and to be worth while such investigations must be lengthy, detailed and objective. Justification for them is found in the words of a leading American geographer who wrote: "A great field of public service awaits those who become proficient in the political geography of the world. They should make intensive field studies in co-operation with historians and economists of each of the danger zones. A better understanding of the causes that may precipitate trouble will go far toward removing the danger of that trouble."[4]

The second illustration is of another type. The word "pattern" has been used frequently in these pages, and it must be admitted that all too often the patterns of the political geographer are like jigsaw puzzles from which some of the pieces are missing. Nevertheless, he commands, in common with his fellow geographers, the use of cartographic methods with which to reproduce his patterns, incomplete as they may be, in maps and diagrams, the construction of which serves two purposes. Data plotted in cartographic form are brought within the range of recognition and assimilation more easily than by mere numerical or literary statement; areas are more readily comparable, and distributions of populations, means of circulation and factors of nodality are more concisely stated and with greater clarity in maps than in any other way.

[1] "Geography and Political Boundaries in Upper Silesia", R. Hartshorne, *Annals of the American Association of Geographers*, Vol. XXIII, 1933.

[2] *Manuel Géographique de Politique Européenne*, J. Ancel, Paris, 1940, Chapters III and IV.

[3] *The Italo–Yugoslav Boundary*, A. E. Moodie, London, 1945.

[4] W. W. Atwood, "The Increasing Significance of Geographical Conditions in the Growth of Nation States", *Annals of the American Association of Geographers*, New York, Vol. XXV, 1935, p. 14.

On the other hand, the selection of data to be mapped and experiments to test their relevance often reveal correlations which might otherwise be overlooked. The simple device of superimposing tracings of various aspects of an area is well-known and frequently provides clues to relationships which might have escaped notice. For whichever of these two purposes maps are constructed, they are one of the most valuable instruments of Political Geography. In passing, attention may be drawn to the production of national atlases with a word of regret that Britain, as yet, possesses the beginnings only of such a record, and to the importance, for detailed studies, of the maps of the official national surveys.

It has often been alleged that statistics can be made to prove anything and that maps can be drawn to illustrate anything. Certainly some of the cartographic illustrations produced by German Geopolitikers, while assuming the form of maps, were gross distortions of known facts. All maps, except those on the largest scales, and they are seldom of much value in Political Geography because they represent small areas, tend to generalize and over-simplify, and, in so doing, are liable to distort, but if these limitations are recognized, and the highest possible accuracy is attained in their construction, then they are an excellent tool. It is not insignificant that government departments and military headquarters are becoming increasingly map-conscious.

Relationships between "backward" peoples and those of Europe or of European origin, in so far as they are determined by political considerations, are a third example of the interests of political geographers. In the past, colonies and other dependencies were generally regarded as mere appendages of the colonial Powers, the main aim of which was to exploit the dependent territories, their people and resources, in the interests of the home country; the advantages gained by the subordinated people were incidental to this process, and particularly where their lands lay in intertropical latitudes the inhabitants were usually regarded as inferior and backward. Hence the differentiation between "white" and "coloured" peoples, which dominated earlier colonial policies and still survives in the prejudices which are observable among both groups, prejudices which have been frequently encouraged for imperial purposes.

Where vast areas were run by comparatively few white administrators and overseers, whose authority rested on the tacit assumption of their superiority, there were probably good social and other reasons for opposing any egalitarian treatment of the "natives", with the result that the long-held political concept of the autocratic rule of a minority group was implanted in the colonies with the modification that the ruling class was of alien origin. The usual justification of this practice was that the natives were inefficient and incapable of governing themselves. This somewhat naïve view was based on the assumption that the European mode of life was the best form of organization or, to be more precise, that the standards and methods of the home country were the most appropriate to any part of the world where it might be expedient to apply them, and overlooked the fact that native societies had evolved their own adaptations to environmental conditions, themselves quite different from those in the habitats of their rulers.

This criticism does not deny the greatness of the European contribution to the material welfare of mankind nor, indeed, to civilization in general. André Siegfried concludes, after visiting several continents, that the genius of the Occident—Europe and North America—is

" . . . le sens de la grande administration: concevoir, organiser, faire marcher de vastes enterprises, dépassant par leur portée l'intérêt particulier et même l'intérêt national, voilà ce dont la plupart des peuples extra-européens, et même plusieurs peuples de l'Europe elle-même, n'ont pas encore prouvé qu'ils fussent capables."[1]

His judgment is a sound one and probably these "vast enterprises", such as the interoceanic canals of Suez and Panama, could not have been brought to fruition by other peoples, but it will not be claimed that colonial policies and achievements were primarily directed in the interests of

[1] A. Siegfried, *Suez–Panama*, Paris, 1945, p. 283.

the native occupants of dependencies however much incidental benefit they may have derived from them. Examples of the subordination of their interests, such as the repressive native policy of the Union of South Africa and the reservation of the best lands to white people in other parts of Africa, are relics of the previously held conception that the natives should occupy the status of "hewers of wood and drawers of water", in the interests of their white rulers.

Two of the greatest colonial Powers introduced modifications of this practice. Britain applied the principle of indirect rule in many parts of its Empire, and France, working along different lines, granted French citizenship, with its privileges and obligations, to the peoples of her colonies, but down to the end of the First World War the relationship between white and coloured peoples—the latter, it will be remembered, constitute the majority of the world's population—were dominated by the gulf which represented the differences implied in the superiority of the former and the inferiority of the latter. With the promulgation of the Wilsonian doctrine of self-determination at the international conferences which took place between 1918 and 1920, the political freedom, which was conferred on the previously subjugated peoples of the Habsburg Empire and other areas, stimulated the desire for similar rights among some of the coloured peoples in the British and other Empires.

A change in outlook was indicated by the adoption of the Mandate System which, nominally at least, was designed to prevent assimilation of the mandated territory which was to be held in trust until its people showed evidence of being able to administer their own affairs. The application of the idea of trusteeship gave rise to varying results, some quite different from the wishes of its sponsors, but it did lay down the basis of a new relationship which has found its latest expression in the establishment of the United Nations Trusteeship Council which consists of representatives of Trustee States and non-Trustee States in equal proportions. At the time of writing, Iraq, Transjordan, Syria and the Lebanon have already acquired independence, India and Pakistan have obtained Dominion status, a similar arrangement is being negotiated with Burma and an enlightened constitution has been recently adopted in Ceylon; the U.S.S.R. is nominally a political union of so-called Autonomous Republics in which regional cultural diversities are encouraged, but economic and strategic matters are co-ordinated in an all-embracing, planned organization which is not only directed from, but imposed by, the central government in Moscow.

There can be no doubt, then, that great progress has been made towards self-government by the backward peoples; in consequence, the idea of their inferiority is in process of transformation, and largely because of the accumulation of knowledge of the conditions under which they live. Studies such as Lord Hailey's *African Survey*, official government reports, including censuses, and the researches of Russian geographers, anthropologists, geologists and others in Soviet Asia, have provided the basic information without which political systems cannot be successfully established except perhaps by the use of military force. Little of this work has been done by political geographers as such, but the subject matter which is being rapidly gathered together gives increasingly valuable foundations for their assessments of world affairs and especially of the relationships between advanced and backward peoples.

These three examples, covering as they do the analysis of the physical and human conditions which underlie the relationships between groups of people, the recognition of the existence of danger areas where maladjustments have not yet been rectified, and the cartographic representation of the results of these studies, indicate some of the main elements in the field of investigation of the political geographer in international affairs. Many aspects of the problems which are inherent in the global political pattern are beyond his competence; the details of legal, technological and ideological matters, for instance, lie outside his scope, nor is it his aim to produce grandiose schemes for the purposes of military conquest. On the other hand, he sees that international affairs are necessarily the results of inter-State relationships conducted on a territorial stage, and will remain so while the world is divided into numerous completely independent political entities. Hence, he is also concerned with the internal affairs, the developed and potential resources and power, the political system and ways of life of the individual States, since they determine their mutual inter-relations to a very great extent.

For centuries, most communities, whatever their form of organization, were largely self-contained social and economic units. Trade between them was mainly in luxury goods, and if, for any reason, commercial intercourse ceased, the communities could survive without undue hardship being suffered by the majority of their members. With the coming of the Industrial Revolution and its associated developments in productivity and circulation, that earlier phase passed away. Since the opening of the nineteenth century, therefore, States have become not only more highly organized internally, but also have grown more closely dependent on each other economically. During that period Britain and France enjoyed immense advantages from their geographical positions, and from their early start in the processes of national consolidation.

It was inevitable, however, that other States should evolve along more or less similar lines to produce rivals, and the competition between them for power destroyed hopes of the success of isolationist policies, because the interests of the competing Powers had become world-wide, yet all the States of the twentieth century have attempted to safeguard their individual interests by erecting barriers against each other. International boundaries became, more than ever before, trespass lines often heavily fortified, but possibly more important were the tariff barriers which every State put up to safeguard its internal economy. The conflict between national and international interests, which had been steadily growing, was brought to a head. The two world wars broke down the barriers temporarily, but in each post-war period reconstruction was hindered by tariff policies.

It is clear that the chief obstacle to global political unity is the existence of States which continue to exercise barrier-like functions in the short-term interests of their inhabitants. Abundant evidence of the recognition of this stumbling-block is provided in the innumerable schemes which have been put forward as means to overcome it. The mistake most of the protagonists of these schemes make lies in demanding their application too quickly. They fail to recognize that the diversities in State organization are the results of a lengthy process of adaptation, that traditions die hard, and that "too much history is remembered". A new world order implies too great a revolution in internal affairs to be rapidly accepted —that is why the League of Nations and the United Nations Organization have been regarded here as experiments. They are not panaceas for the overnight solution of world problems; only a Utopian or a rash idealist would expect them to succeed at the first attempt. Knowledge of the internal political geography of States suggests that a completely successful world order will be achieved only by a slow process of adjustment which will make necessary the sacrifice of some of the sovereign powers of each and every State. This, in its turn, demands the growth of favourable, informed, public opinion, because, if the new order is not freely accepted, it will not be likely to survive.

Two final suggestions may be made here. First, the removal of the fear of war would probably facilitate the growth of a new order, because many of the barriers erected by States are the outcome of policies based on fear and suspicion of aggression. Given a century of peace, the next generation but one might find itself living in an orderly world society from which the dangers of recurrent total warfare had been eliminated. While it is true that the two world wars undoubtedly exercised a stimulating effect on the minds of men with regard to new political arrangements in the world, they have surely demonstrated the futility of attempted imposition of new orders by military force. Second, it may be suggested that the ultimate aim of a free association of all peoples, white and coloured, may be more easily attained after regional groupings of States, such as those indicated in Chapter IV, have been tried.

The difficulties even in such arrangements are great. It is no easy matter to modify trade associations and agreements, as the Geneva Conference on tariffs in 1947 showed, and Customs Unions necessitate more alterations in internal affairs than is usually suspected. Much will depend on the degree of success with which individual States weather the economic storms of the next five to ten years. If the after-effects of two world wars in one generation are overcome, the existence of States as independent units may be prolonged for a considerable period, but this will not alter the fundamental factor that the present political system, if it may be called such, is inadequate to meet the requirements of a united world society. The stage is set for the performance of the greatest political drama in history. The leading characters are the statesmen of all nations, but the interplay of forces in the drama are conditioned by the physical character of the stage, whether the setting of a particular scene is located in London, Washington or Moscow.

INDEX

ACCESS to sea, 119–20
Age of Discovery, 68, 105, 106
Air transport, 129–32
Alsace, 79, 169
Ancel, J., 78, 80, 169
Appalachians, 75
Atwood, W. W., 169
Australia, 159
Azcárate, P. de, 15, 101

"BACKWARD" Peoples, 170–73
Barcelona Agreement, 119
Basch, A., 122
Basques, 89
Belgium, 152
Blache, V. de la., 47, 105, 123
Boggs, S. W., 73, 81, 84–5, 95, 99
Brunhes, J., 124

CANADA, 48–9, 159
Capital cities, 157–60
Capot-Rey, 109, 125, 132
Carr-Saunders, Sir A. M., 134, 140, 143, 148
Censuses, 14, 133
Centralization, 54–5, 108
China, 106, 115, 134, 140, 142
City States, 23
Climate, 35–6, 46–8, 109
Colonial Empires, 39–41
Conference System, 114
"Conquest of Nature", 10
Continental circulation, 120–6
Conurbations, 152
Cornish, V., 158
Czechoslovakia, 28, 119

DANUBE, 94, 125
Dark Ages, 23
Demangeon, A., 16, 163
Determinism, 8, 21
Dickinson, R. E., 156

EAST, W. G., 134

Economic Imperialism, 26, 65–6
Economic nationalism, 30–1, 121
Egypt, 44, 94
Elbe, 94
Emigration, 141, 143
"Encirclement", 36
Ethnic groups, 51–2

FAWCETT, C. B., 60, 124, 133, 152, 156, 161
Federal States, 159
Feudal System, 24, 70, 105
Fleure, H. F., 142, 150, 155
France, 37, 46, 48, 74, 138, 149
Freedom of the air, 130, 131
Freedom of the seas, 113

GEOMETRICAL boundaries, 98–9
Geopolitik, 15–7, 163
Germany, 36–7, 122, 138
Gilbert, E. W., 56, 156
Glass, D. V., 138, 145
Goblet, Y., 80
Great Britain, 35, 61–2, 118, 147–8, 152, 153
Great Powers, 24–5
Greece, 23 114

HARTSHORNE, R., 169
Haushofer, 16
Heartland, 60–1

IMPERIALISM, 64–5, 67
India, 10, 11, 140, 142
Industrialization, 31, 42, 141, 151
Italy, 17, 74, 138
Internal divisions of States, 55–6
Interoceanic canals, 117, 171
Iraq, 44

JEFFERSON, M., 111
Jones, S. B., 74
Jugoslavia, 28, 53, 119–20
Julian Region, 78

LANDRY, A., 144
Language, 51–3
Lattimore, O., 142
League of Nations, 32, 64, 166
Location, 26, 35, 37
Lorimer, F., 153, 154

MACKINDER, Sir H., 60, 69, 113
Man-power, 50, 147–9
Mance, O., 112, 114, 128
Mandate System, 172
Maps, 169–70
Martin, L., 97
Median line, 95, 96
Mediterranean Sea, 13, 104
Middle Zone of Europe, 29, 75
Morphology of oceans, 116–8

NATIONALISM, 26–8, 87, 109, 141
Navigable channel, 95–6
Norway, 114
Notestein, F. W., 137
Nuclear areas, 37–8, 94, 158

OCEANIC circulation, 112
Oppenheim, L., 111
Optimum population, 144–5

PACT of Rome of 1924, 96
Physical basis of States, 41–9
Physical features as boundaries, 87–97
Population, 49–50, 133–144; distribution, 149–157; policies, 138, 144–6; pressure, 137
Primitive societies, 22

Poland, 29

RATZEL, 16
Regional capitals, 160–2
Regional groupings, 69–71
Religion, 53–4
Reproduction rates, 137–8, 140, 146
Rhine, 74, 94
Rivers, 43–5
Rome, 164

SAUCERMAN, S., 29, 74
Seaboards, 45–6
Self-determination, 28–30, 100
Siegfried, A., 117, 163, 171
Size of States, 37–41
Sovereignty, 20, 24, 54, 59, 125

TAYLOR, E. G. R., 167
Territorial expansion, 25–6
Transhumance, 89, 92

UNITED Nations Organization, 32, 64, 80, 166, 172, 175
Urbanization, 151–7
U.S.A., 38–9, 48, 116, 127, 154, 159
U.S.S.R., 25, 37–9, 58, 62–4, 85, 119, 123, 153–4, 173

VALKENBURG, S. van, 21

WATERSHEDS, 92
Whittlesey, D., 16
Wireless telegraphy, 11, 111, 126